KEEPING HEART

ooooo

Library of Congress Control Number: 2017916160

ISBN: 978-0-9843991-9-2

Spiritual Root System™ and The Eight Feelings™ are trademarked by Sage Hill, LLC.

Edited by Tennyson Dodd.

Cover design by Bekah Wertz Design.
Interior design by Bekah Wertz Design.

www.sagehillresources.com

KEEPING

HEART

∞∞∞

A series of reflections on the art of
LIVING FULLY

∞∞∞

BY CHIP DODD

CONTENTS

ooooo

INTRODUCTION

ooooo

Some time ago, I was talking to a small group about our hearts. During this group, I spoke of the heart's characteristics, value, purpose, movements, and the power of its presence in our lives. At some point in the discussion that night, I stated that humans are created as emotional and spiritual creatures, created to do one thing in this life: live fully. I mentioned that a specific need arises when we desire to live fully — the need to keep heart in the midst of the rough and tumble rhythm of our lives.

After I used this phrase, someone asked me a simple and profound question: What does it mean to "keep heart"?

I paused, and then answered the question by saying that "keep heart" is shorthand for many vital capacities. Keeping heart is a way to say stay involved in life emotionally and spiritually — to continue caring, come what may — and to participate fully in life with our hands, heads, and especially with our hearts.

These were just a few shorthand answers to a very important question in a quest to live fully. After I left that group, I wanted to answer that question more fully. The result is this series of reflections. It is dedicated to that person who asked the question and to anyone else who wants to know more about what it means to "keep heart."

At its foundational core, keeping heart means to grow our inborn emotional and spiritual makeup to maturity. We were born with all we need, in rudimentary forms, to live life well. We were born with courage — full-hearted participation. We were born with faith — sure of what we hoped for, and certain of what we did not see. We were born working — giving our hands, head, and heart to what matters to us. We were also born in need, dependent upon others to join with us to grow into who we have been created to become. These rudimentary expressions of creation are to be preserved and grown through relationship.

We've been created to grow through relationship with ourselves, others, and God, as we face the pain of loss and the joy of celebration together. We are created to keep the heart of how we were born, amid a world of influences that would say that withholding our courage, giving up faith, and reducing life to the labor of survival alone, is the wiser course.

How do we live courageously, faithfully, and dutifully with heart? We live the courage, faith, and commitments involved in "keeping heart" by feeling our core feelings, telling the truth about them, and giving it all to the process.

When I mention "feeling our core feelings", I am not talking about reactions to feelings or making demands that someone "fix" our feelings. On the contrary, I mean the continuous confession of our feelings in relationship with others we trust, which allows us to respond to life truthfully, come what may.

Telling the truth about our feelings in relationship leads us to living in the process. And the process is the way life works, with or without our involvement. We do not have control of life; rather, we are called to live fully in it without all the answers, and certainly without the control we desire to possess. We live in the process well by keeping heart.

Discussing the feelings and virtues involved in keeping heart brings many more questions to the surface: How do I live fully? What is courage? What am I created to be like? How will I know? What difference will it make? What are core feelings? What is the truth? How do we live the truth? How do I persevere?

I started this series of reflections to continue speaking into the keeping heart question, and the questions that naturally follow, the ones that I think are significant in the journey toward full life.

The reason I say "speak into" is because we live the questions in our daily lives, which means these questions can't simply be answered and then settled forever. Keeping heart helps us live the questions of life until we are no longer here. It does not lead us to the answers for all of life's problems to protect us from struggle.

You may read this series however you wish. You may read it from front to back, back to front, or randomly pick any paragraph. Nevertheless, I have a suggestion for how to read it based on how it was constructed.

The following paragraphs offer a series of separately cut stones or pearls, so to speak. In other words, the book does not flow linearly from front to back. Rather, the paragraphs are clustered together based on central themes. Each title represents stand alone paragraphs that can be read as a singular meditation on a given topic. However, you may also string the pearlesque paragraphs together, letting the eyes of the heart gather them. In doing this, you will create a full strand of great value, a gift both to your heart and a potential gift to be given. I think you'll find the strand to be a treasure for your heart, a gift for your mind, and strength in daily life.

The following reflections, read together or separately, allow us to understand and grasp more of what it means to "keep heart." We can live more fully, love more deeply, and lead more substantively when we do. When you read any of the following paragraphs, it will help you open the door to living in a way that leaves something behind of worth for others, because these short reflections let us see who we are made to be and do what we are made to do.

CHAPTER ONE

KEEPING HEART

∞∞

HOW WE ARE CREATED

We are created to live fully as emotional and spiritual creatures. We can only be fully alive in emotional and spiritual relationship with ourselves (our heads with our hearts), others (one heart with another heart), and God (our hearts with God). We are born crying out for life, and our cries are stilled in the arms of a mother and then a father. We are born reaching out for connection, a need that is met when a newborn connects to the skin of a caregiver. We are born taking life in, reaching for nourishment that will fill and comfort.

When the cry out, reach out, and the taking-in are met in relationship with the mother, father, and other caregivers, a baby's physiology and heart become regulated through relational connections. This feeds an infant's body and also meets the heart's craving for belonging and mattering. Belonging and mattering allow the child to remain open in heart and action as they cry out, reach out, and take in the food of life and relationship in increasingly more complex and exploratory ways.

As the child develops, the infant's cry out becomes an expression of grief at life's inevitable pains and frustrations. The reach out becomes the willingness to take the risk to explore what life has to offer. The taking in becomes a willingness to experience life on life's terms, as we begin to know that life offers the nourishment that we seek. If a child is nurtured to operate from the context of relational belonging and mattering, they will trust their inborn ability to feel their feelings about life, tell the truth about their inner experiences, and give themselves to relationships that value the expressions of the heart.

HEART

The heart is the center of one's being. Out of the heart we feel, need, desire, long, and hope. The heart is comprised of these five core areas, which allow us to grow and connect, imagine and grieve, attach and love. The heart is the origin of our identification with each other and the place from which we become unique. It is the home from which we care and make ourselves known. The heart is the place from which we experience life and through which we direct our wills. It is the seat of our emotional constitution and home of the universal language that all humans are created to speak. It is the birthplace and homestead of courage. The heart is also the place of God's greatest concern for us. For if we do not live out of our hearts, and if God does not live within our hearts, we are adrift. We live detached from how we are created, who we are created to become, whose we are created to be, and what we are created to do.

HEART'S SUBSTANCE

The heart consists of five roots, or primary characteristics, that grow into a powerful fruit-bearing tree when planted in the soil of relationship. The roots are feelings, needs, longings, desire, and hope. If the roots are given the food of emotional and spiritual nourishment, the heart hydrates and oxygenates who a person is created to become. The roots that are nourished become the fruits of abundance. These fruits express the generative, creative freedom of being fully alive. These fruits are not about production as much as expression of one's identity, interests, and creativity.

TRUTH

Sentio ergo sum is the inborn truth of human beings: I feel or experience the center of my being; therefore, I am. That truth does not change with age or the development of rational abilities and power. *Cogito ergo sum* is not so true: I think; therefore, I am. If we use *cogito ergo sum* as the starting point to define who we are, we are in error. Being creatures made with the faculty of reason does not mean that reason is the master of the non-rational emotional world within us. On the contrary, our thoughts are made to be tools we use to express the inborn primacy of the heart. The thinking brain's task is twofold: to articulate our emotional and spiritual experiences and to figure out the myriad tasks of daily life, from stopping at red lights to neurosurgery. We are created to use our thoughts to express the heart and its makeup, not to conquer the heart. The truth of how we are created as emotional and spiritual creatures is not simply a nuisance of feelings, needs, longings, desire and hope rattling around as a holdover from more primitive times. We do not merely need to tolerate or attempt to master these characteristics of the heart. We are created to live with our hearts, heads, and hands integrated in the service of ourselves, others, and God.

GOD AND HEART

God values the heart and "keeping heart" greatly. The heart is referred to almost a thousand times in the Bible. The heart is referred to more than spirit, soul, or mind. Moreover, the countless uses of its synonyms in the Bible — courage, stand firm, confidence, and willingness as matters of the heart — further speak to the value of the heart to God and, therefore, to our lives. Being able to trust, have faith, stand firm, have courage, love, or "keep heart" in the midst of a life that is often filled with sadness and tragedy is something we must seek to know and treasure. God calls us into such a real and truthful life. Without our hearts being alive to God's presence and faithfulness, we cannot live fully. We will merely exist and survive disconnected and adrift, which runs counter to what we are created to imagine and how we are created to live.

IMAGO DEI

The capacity to imagine flows through the heart. We carry within us the Imago Dei, and thus we are the image bearers of God. We are created in God's image, and come to know our creation, the roots of who we are, in the Imago Dei. We are not God, but creatures created to bear the image of God. As such, we are relational and created to connect. We are also created to create and participate in whatever is true, noble, right, pure, lovely, admirable, excellent, or praiseworthy. We express our image bearing when participating in the good, in all of its rich and multiple expressions.

BEING HUMAN

When we are born, we cry out for care, reach out for attachment, and suck in food of life with freedom of heart. These movements occur without contempt for the absolute neediness they express. We are created or "pre-designed" to seek and find fulfillment in relationship. Our essential created nature is relational. Our early movements toward caretakers as infants is perhaps the original example of how we are created to connect, join, and attach relationally as emotional and spiritual creatures. We are born powerless over this truth about us. For human beings, fulfillment comes from reaching for and being in relationship with ourselves, others, and God.

CHILDREN

Children are born with the incipient, joyous expression of what become grownup versions of courage, faith, and work. These words are often considered to be not of the child's world. They are considered to be only a part of the adult world of character development, religion, and maturity. However, I want to offer a consideration of these terms in relation to the heart of human beings — the rudiments of what will become mature courage, faith, and work in a healthy grownup. Nevertheless, the essentials of these things are inborn. Children bring full-hearted participation to life — courage. They are sure of what they hope for, and they are certain that what they do not yet see — faith. They give their hands, head, and heart to pursuing life and its fulfillment — work. Through the growth of heart, the child's courage becomes the grownup's ability to remain firm in the face of tenuous or frightening situations.

Emotional and spiritual experiences of the heart convert childlike certainty of what is unseen into a persistent faith in the face of evidence that suggests its foolishness. The childhood capacity for work is made to become more than the adult's curse of labor, because work can involve the imagination and care of expending great energy on doing what matters to us. These three characteristics develop fully when fed through relationship with others and God. If nurtured well, they become expressions of living fully, loving deeply, and leading well.

AFFIRMATION AND CONFIRMATION

We are born to grow into who we are created to become. We do so through having our hearts affirmed and confirmed by caretakers. Affirmation says "yes" to who we are as emotional and spiritual creatures. Confirmation multiplies affirmation's "yes" by repeating it. In a world that generally does not support the vulnerability of desire and the courage to express it, we are in desperate need to be affirmed and confirmed in heart. Affirmation and confirmation from caregivers feeds the two primary needs in the child to belong and to matter. When we are fed well, we have a great opportunity to grow fully into who we were created to become.

WHAT CHILDREN WANT

Children really have only a few essential questions of caregivers: Will you grow up with me? Will you help me become grown up? Will you live in the struggle of remaining present with me? Children need to be able to take the affirmative answers to these questions for granted, and only later in life find great gratitude in them being answered well. Children do not demand perfection, even though they cry when imperfection is discovered. They do attempt to demand, however, the persistent presence of the caregiver. The presence they crave, importantly, is a presence of heart, not a presence of perfection. A child is born expressing heart, and they want the caregiver to "keep heart" and help them do the same in a world that can pull us away from who we are created to be.

POWERLESSNESS

We are powerless over being created to operate in a certain way. Just like trees are powerless over needing to seek water, humans find their "water" in relationship with self, others, and God. Powerlessness is not negative or an insult. However, many of us have a tremendously difficult time facing and living into the powerlessness of how we are created. The vulnerability it takes to live relationally is terrifying for many of us because we have been deeply wounded in past relationships. The struggle with powerlessness for humans, therefore, is that we have experienced great pains that make us wish not to be powerless over needing to reach from our hearts to the water of relationship. This pain often impels us to willfully go against our relational pre-design as a form of protection. But the protection eventually isolates our hearts from relationship.

Attempting to gain control over our powerlessness often involves the use of willpower to stymie, neglect, or deny the emotional and spiritual makeup of our hearts. In the end, all of our attempts to live without reaching for relationship out of the heart prove fruitless. Just like trees are powerless over needing to seek water, humans find their water in relationship with self, others, and God. Human powerlessness is a paradoxical opportunity or invitation to live how we've been created, as emotional and spiritual creatures destined for relationship. It takes tremendous courage to live into our powerlessness. We never get over being powerless as humans — needy, desirous, hopeful, harmful, helpful, imaginative, relational and created. In acknowledging these truths, we can surrender daily to this reality as a way to live how we are created day in and day out. Daily surrender to and acceptance of our powerlessness sets us free to live in relationship with the truthful vulnerability of our hearts.

WILL POWER

We are born powerless over how we are created to feel, need, desire, long and hope. All of these characteristics of the heart move us toward relational living. Having described the importance of powerlessness in keeping heart, it is also necessary to articulate the proper place of willpower in a life of heart. Simply, we are created to grow into people who use willpower to live fully, love deeply, and lead well. The will is meant to be submitted to our feelings, needs, desire, longings, hope, imaginings, dreams and so on. Willpower is intended to serve the heart, not dominate it, as is often the case. Proper use of willpower is developed through caregivers who help us fortify the will to keep heart. The will to keep heart is sustained, not by emphasizing willpower, but by caregivers affirming and confirming the makeup of the heart. Doing so allows the will to be used to express the heart, rather than developing the use of willpower to hide the heart. So often, we tragically learn to use willpower to refuse the voice of our hearts. The will of the human being is made to serve the heart, not to supersede it.

COURAGE

Having courage and "keeping heart" are virtually synonymous. The Latin word *cor* means heart and is the root word for the English word courage. *Cor* means the center of one's person, the essential makeup or heart of a person. We are born with a core, out of which we have courage: full-hearted participation and the complete offering of ourselves to life and living, the capacity to be "all in". We are born offering our feelings, needs, longings, desire, and hope to caregivers. We cannot do otherwise at birth. When we are young, we cannot defend ourselves from reaching for connection, showing our neediness, or expressing our dependence. We don't develop this kind of courage; it is inborn. We do, however, have to fight to keep it. We need to be encouraged by connection with trusted others, so that we have our courage reinvigorated to continually offer our feelings, needs, longings, desire, and hope to God's process. We come out of the womb as courageous emotional and spiritual creatures, created to do one thing — live fully. And we cannot live fully unless we do so with others and remain connected to God, both of whom nurture the courage to keep heart in a tragic place.

RESPONSE ABILITY

Response ability is the capacity to have feelings, express needs, apply desire, accept longings and keep hope. We are able to use our responses to ourselves, others, and God to be known. Being known allows us to connect, attach, and live as we are created to live. The response from within and the ability to communicate our internal experiences is the true normal at birth, the true normal of how we grow, and the true normal of how the grownup keeps going forward.

INTEGRITY AS A NATURAL OUTGROWTH OF RESPONSE ABILITY

Integrity is the consistent alignment of word and deed. When a person lives congruently, they have the opportunity to become credible and trustworthy. A person of integrity is someone who can be trusted to be truthful. Integrity does not mean that a person is an open book all of the time. Moreso, it is not concerned with perfection or making the correct decision. Rather, living with integrity involves choosing a direction that one can live toward. A person who lives integrity has practiced response ability as a way to walk the path of living. While living with a focus of response ability, they have become responsible. They tend to be trusted, relied upon, and cared about openly. What can limit the development of integrity is that most of us are taught that responsibility means something other than keeping and growing the response ability of the heart. So often, the internal voice of the heart is silenced so that a person appears responsible in its common and tragic use of the word. When responsible means that a person denies their internal experience, becomes an actor for others' approval to be thought of as dependable or valuable, and spends their days in holding up a front, this person, sadly, may be following a belief of integrity that is actually incongruity. The heart must not be missed as the beginning point of integrity.

GROWTH

We are designed to be able to learn how to live and grow as emotional and spiritual creatures. We are even designed to be able to do so in a place that requires great struggle and is often tragic. Growth occurs from the inside out by developing our ability to live in relationship with self, others, and God. As I have said, we are born with our hearts searching for emotional and spiritual fulfillment. At birth, however, we are unaware that searching for fulfillment with our hearts is a vulnerable state in which great harm can and does occur.

Once we discover that vulnerability of heart is one of the birthplaces of great pain, we tend to do what we can to avoid vulnerability, even though we are created to be vulnerable. For good reason, we become conflicted about risking the vulnerability of our hearts with others and God. The "picture" we had of how life could be is thrown into conflict after we discover how reality differs from our original hopes. Yet, in order to continue to grow from the inside out, we must learn to risk being vulnerable enough to be hurt again, as this state of vulnerability is also how we get fulfilled emotionally and spiritually. Even though vulnerability is so often associated with the negative, we must learn to see that vulnerability is not stupid, weak, wrong, or a condition of birth that ends with so-called maturity. A willingness to be vulnerable for the sake of fulfillment actually expresses a courageous willingness to be wounded in relationship with the knowledge that being wounded is inevitable, though not the last word. The vulnerability exposed by craving full life in relationship is the expression of creation itself pursuing its own fulfillment in us, the human being following God's thoughtfulness and goodness. We do not need to change how we are born. We must grow into who we are born to become — vulnerable creatures of heart — if we are to fully participate in life.

FULFILLMENT

Humans are created to experience fulfillment in relationship, to care and be cared about. It is important to note that fulfillment is not a place that we can finally reach on this earth. It's not a project we can simply complete and then remain fulfilled forever. Fulfillment, rather, is a state we are created to search for without ever being able to completely attain it during this life. Just as after a delicious meal we will soon be hungry again, relational fulfillment is a food that we need to feed on continuously. Relational fulfillment, then, obviously is not a place we reach in which we will never have to need, struggle, or have tears again. Being created for fulfillment, quite paradoxically, calls us to pursue a life that we can never have completely in this world. Nevertheless, the heart calls us to pursue it. Simply, we are created to seek fullness in relationship with ourselves, others, and God while living in a place of limitation.

Relational connection, bonding, and expression are the foods of growth and fulfillment for human beings. These foods feed our "pre-design" as emotional and spiritual beings created for relationship. Being nurtured with relational connection sets us free to celebrate life's great treasures and keeps us alive during seasons of tremendous heartache. Without the love and care of others, we would not be able to bear our grief or joy, as both are meant to be experienced and shared in relationship with others and God.

YES

We are created to be able to say a full-hearted "yes" to life on life's terms. To do so requires that we risk a courageous, vulnerable participation in life. We have to develop the willingness to live in an open-hearted way, trusting that vulnerability is the key to fulfillment, and not only a form of getting harmed. We are prepared to pursue life to its fullest when we can live well even when our affirmation of life ends in pain. An ability to say "yes" to life with the awareness that it can, so to speak, be damaged by loss or other pains, is a tremendous example of living in the process. We leave the process when we develop compulsive actions oriented around demanding that our "yes" to life be affirmed by life. When we do this, we have left life on life's terms behind for our own vision of how life should work. The compulsive actions are an attempt to have fulfillment without having to pay the price of fully feeling what comes with being courageous and vulnerable. Fulfillment is always linked to surrendering to the process of life on life's terms with full-hearted participation and a willingness to be hurt.

LOVE'S DEMAND

To love requires that we be willing to experience pain, whether we love our spouses, our children, our friends, or God. With love comes the paradoxical struggle of perseverance and powerlessness. In love we experience the hunger, desire, wish, yearning, longing, hoping of love's capacity to persevere. We also experience the inability to control others in this life and life itself. Love cannot be lived well if it is a force that would control. To live this paradox requires great courage — giving one's heart away that may not be received or may entail great loss. Avoiding love's demand, though, requires that we hide our hearts, and therefore remove ourselves from living this life. We must place who we truly are in a place of isolation, removed from the light of living. And the misery of isolation will make a person invulnerable to the ache of care, impenetrable to the offer of mercy, hardened against the tears of joy. Love demands the willingness to be vulnerable, and to suffer its inevitabilities. It does mean wounds; it does mean powerlessness; it does mean joy. What love costs is always less than the price of not facing its demand.

HEART'S STRENGTH IN LOVE

Love doesn't work like lust. Love can tolerate, and even thrive, during discomfort. We are born craving that which becomes love through good enough relational care. However, through a number of ways, we develop contempt of the heart's neediness. This contempt so often drives us to distance ourselves from living in the craving to be loved and to love, so we settle for lust instead. Lust exposes an impaired attempt to get legitimate needs met through illegitimate means. It is an attempt to escape the realities of vulnerability. Mature love requires that we develop a willingness to live in pain for something or someone that is greater than pain. Without help to persevere in heart amidst the pain of living, we attempt to resign from the way the heart works — vulnerable, needy, powerless. Love requires great strength of heart, and therefore the heart is what requires a preponderance of attention from loved ones and God. The risk of love requires us to give all of our hearts to someone or something without having control of the results.

LIVING FROM THE INSIDE OUTWARDS

As a person thinks in their heart, so is the person, states the ancient proverb. The heart communicates the feelings, needs, longings, desire and hope of the experience of being human. Then, the thought processes communicate the heart in ideas, imagination, dreams, yearnings, feelings, desire, longings, hopes, the experience of thinking, planning, and taking action in response ability. The face and body are created to present the credible outward expression of the inward disposition. In expressing our inner disposition, we create a potential for a relational identification with another or God. The process of living who we are made to be makes us available in sincere ways to relational connection and fulfillment of many different kinds.

ORDER OF LIVING

We are created to participate in a certain order of living:

1. God

2. Self

3. Loved Ones

4. Others.

God has created the heart as an emotional and spiritual core within each of us that actually needs the God who made us. In order to love well those who we love much, we must draw nutrients from a God who feeds our hearts, gives us strength, and helps shape our purpose and character through relationship with Him. Simply, we cannot give what we do not have. We need God to live beyond our defensiveness, and to supply us with strength, purpose and love beyond our abilities. To be able to have what we wish to offer, we must draw on God and others to fill the self so that it may overflow into the lives of loved ones. Following God, and one's heart that draws from God, comes whomever we love beyond and more than others. That person, and those people, are our people, and they look to us for what they do not have. To grow into someone who can give and receive love, others we love must be third, and we must be third to them to receive their best.

THE PROCESS

The process of living fully, loving deeply and leading well requires that we surrender to how life on life's terms works. Simply, we do not have control of life. We are, nevertheless, born to live fully in life without all the answers, and certainly without omnipotent control. We can live life on life's terms by surrendering to the process. We do so by keeping heart amid all the pain and struggle of creaturely life. We have been created to bring ourselves to the process of living fully in a particular pathway that has been traveled by many before us. Surrendering to this process has three movements. The first is **Being** who we are created to be as relational creatures. **Being** then leads to **Doing** what we are created to do, meaning we participate in the actions that lead to dreams coming to reality. Lastly, **Being** and **Doing** develop into **Having** what we are created to have, the fulfillment of having offered ourselves to living, loving, and leading. If we are nurtured to keep heart, we can surrender to a mission greater than ourselves and experience the gratification of harvesting the fruits of hearts.

MORE ON THE PROCESS

Being, Doing, and **Having** are the movements of how the process works for our fulfillment amid all the vicissitudes of life. This is an inside out form of growth and life. We respond to life as we are created — **Being**. We take action according to our internal awareness and makeup — **Doing**. We attain the experiences of life that create relational and experiential fulfillments—**Having**. **Being, Doing,** and **Having** are the ways to live fully in a life outside of our control. However, all too often, we get swept up in attempts to take control of the process, refusing life on life's terms. In doing so, we adopt an inverted way of living based on performance and control.

Once a performance-based existence "takes over," for the sake of survival, we can get trapped in the assumption that if we **Do** enough, we will **Have** enough to be acknowledged as **Being** someone of worth. The performance value system is an attempt to have control over life and control over our neediness of others and God. It is an impaired outcome of our early dissociation from our feelings, needs, longings, desire, and hope — our **Being**. **Do-Have-Be** can easily displace **Be-Do-Have**. We will always partially live in conflict with surrendering to life on its own terms. It's hard to do — we all want more control than we have. The great tragedy, though, is when our hearts become hardened against surrendering to or accepting that there is a process that is greater than us, yet one in which we can fully and humbly struggle to participate in.

CHAPTER TWO

THE STRUGGLE FOR CONNECTION

ooooo

SEPARATION FROM HEART

As we develop cognitively throughout childhood and further on, most of us will become, to some degree, separated from our hearts. When separation from our hearts occurs, our thoughts are used to suppress the heart rather than express the heart.

In order to suppress the heart, we often begin practicing thoughts of judgment against ourselves. We assess ourselves with the "low grades" of bad, stupid or weak for having feelings, needs, desire, longings or hope. And, by extension, we minimize the dreams, wishes, and imaginings that grow out of the heart's core characteristics. Believing that the heart is ridiculous or foolish tends to be the only explanation a child can conclude about the unnourished heart. The only offering they can bring to relationships are feelings, needs, desire, longings, and hope; therefore, something must be reproachable about the true self. Again, what is not affirmed by the caregiver is often discarded by the one in need of care.

The good news, however, is that what we tried to discard through judgment has actually been stored. Our hearts await our return, or reassociation, so we can be restored to who we are created to be and become. This reassociation happens when we use our thought processes to listen to the heart rather than grade it.

SICKNESS

We become isolative, ignorant, and sick when the heart becomes subordinated to the functions that are created to serve the expression of the heart. The brain, stomach, skin, and genitals are to serve the heart's fulfillment in relational ways — not replace or supersede the way we are created. Isolation occurs when one denies and dissociates from the heart. Ignorance is a practice we develop by ignoring our hearts. We eventually become sick when we use our stomachs, brains, skin, and genitals to do the work of the heart. Disorders of eating, fantasies of escaping reality, cutting, alcohol, thrill seeking, sexual compulsion, demands, obsession on security, and religious legalism are just a few examples of attempts to quell the heart's neediness in counterfeit ways. All of these experiences are means to feed the heart while at the same time denying its neediness. Existing in such chronic conflict eventually makes us sick. The sickness develops through our inability to live in relationship with our own hearts, with others, and God. The tragic paradox is that which did protect us, hiding the heart, becomes the manner in which we ultimately harm ourselves.

COMPULSION TO AVOID HEART

All compulsive or addictive reactions follow a predictable downward course: a refusal to experience the heart, a lust for self-sufficiency, sustained attempts to avoid feeling life on life's terms, deepening despair, attempts to change because of despair, a reliance on will power to exact change, subsequent failure, and finally... apathy toward one's self and the assumption of apathy in others and God.

Self-cures that are used to avoid feeling, needing, desiring, longing and hoping can become a compulsive avoidance of the heart. No matter how much a person experiences relief from feelings by using a multitude of self-cures, whether they be alcohol, narcotics, sex, risk-taking, or exercise, there is no cure that allows one to avoid the heart forever. In avoiding the heart by whatever means, one has an experience of relief that eventually fades, leaving him or her in the same position they were in beforehand.

Our chosen ways to escape what the heart is feeling become repetitious over time, as we remember how that method has aided our getaway previously. Sadly, this cycle is repeated continuously in order to avoid the voice of the heart that continues to whisper even in the depths of our attempts to stifle it.

DISSOCIATION AND DENIAL

Dissociation and denial are two ways we can protect our hearts from intense emotional and spiritual anguish. These defenses are often meant to help us navigate specific types of pain at our own pace. The great tragedy, however, is that they often become automatic ways of responding to all emotional pain, leaving us distant from our hearts for long, long periods of time.

To begin, these defenses work in tandem, as dissociation is necessary for denial to remain operational. Dissociation is a distancing from one's awareness of the language of the heart as a form of protection from multiple forms of emotional pain. While it is protective, dissociation is self-rejecting. It says, "I no longer associate with this person, the one who is vulnerable to feeling, needing, desiring, longing, and hoping."

Denial defends us from seeing what is actually happening around us. While it is protective, denial is also self-rejecting. It says, "I do not see so that I will not feel; therefore, everything is okay." When we are dissociated and in denial, the desire to have a full life does not go away altogether. However, we now wish to have a full life without having to involve the heart of who we really are.

Returning to the heart requires some significant work after the protective walls of dissociation and denial are constructed. The deconstruction usually occurs when life becomes so overwhelming that denial and dissociation no longer work. When these defenses can no longer protect us from what we are avoiding, a great opportunity has arrived.

REACTIVITY

At an early age, most of us learn to hide, deny, or dissociate from our God-created "response-ability". In doing so, we become reactive and attempt to take too much control of our lives and the people in them.

These maneuvers leave us living life backwards: we do so we can have and thus be. A life that follows a **Do-Have-Be** mantra is actually lived as a series of reactions. Reactions are actions based upon the actions of others. In other words, one's attitudes and behaviors are not his or her own as much as they are opinions and actions we learn to take in order to fit in with powerful and scary people. When we fall into living life backwards, we live so that others will worship us, like us, fear us, be jealous of the stuff we gather, never leave us, desire to copy us, and on and on.

When we lose the trust in and capacity for response ability, **Be-Do-Have** is subordinated to the reactivity of **Do-Have-Be**. Most of the time, we do not even realize we are living in reactivity. We are simply and tragically following the rules we made up to be lovable in an unsafe world. These made up rules often carry the illusion that performance will create the desired end of getting to live in relationship with self, others, and God.

When living under the guidance of reactive rules, we ultimately live in a way that never allows us to be known.

Because we are created to be known from within, if we do not live from our hearts, we cannot experience true fulfillment.

COMPULSION

Once we lose contact with our hearts, there is a tendency for compulsive approval-seeking to replace the true normal of birth. When our behavior no longer follows the pattern of be-do-have, and we instead live in a reactive way, we suppress how God created us and distrust the lives we are created to have. Through a variety of ways, we are led to believe we work for our sense of worth or inner-security, instead of our worth being something we are born with. This misconceived, though understandable, belief leads to a cycle of working hard in an attempt to gain a sense of worth someday. Many of us become very good at using our reactivity to gain temporary feelings of security, whether that be from the praise of others or a variety of mood-altering options.

Unfortunately, feelings of security that are not created through relationship with self, others, and God have a fleeting quality. The temporary nature of this "security" forces us to compulsively search for the next person or thing that will make us feel that we belong and matter. Compulsively seeking the next self-cure eventually leaves us empty and exhausted. We end up in a cycle of acting compulsively in order to avoid the very emptiness compulsion creates.

Furthermore, the condition of being separated from our true selves and working cyclically and chronically to have a sense of worth creates a state of anxiety in us. We become anxious because we are trying to create a secure world for ourselves by controlling the people and things in our lives that are inherently outside of our control. To put it simply, not living out of our hearts creates a life of unease, often made up of anxiety, compulsive satisfaction seeking, and feelings of emptiness.

No matter how much we achieve, an unfulfilled place will remain within our hearts that is made to be touched by relational belonging. Doing takes over being, and we lose recognition of ourselves as feeling creatures. We have to keep doing as a way to keep distance from our feelings, which sparks anxiety rather than expression.

INCONGRUITY

The ability to keep what we feel in our hearts from showing on our faces is called incongruity. We learn to hide our hearts through the use of our faces and actions. In doing so, we mask or deny our own vulnerability in order to remain safe in a dangerous environment. Over time, our faces can become like masks that keep our internal or emotional state from being seen by others. Sometimes, we can become so accustomed to hiding our feelings from others that we no longer realize we are doing so. That condition is reflexive and is rooted in denial. When this happens, we are not even aware of what's going on in our own hearts.

An incongruous life separates us from self, others, and God. The capacity to forego reflexive reactivity and instead, live in response-ability by showing the truth of our hearts, is a vital ability in the quest to live fully and love deeply.

WILL AS REFUSAL OF HEART OR EXPRESSION OF HEART

If the heart becomes subordinated to willpower, we use our will to refuse the truth of our hearts, instead of using the will to permit the expression of our hearts. The will to hide our hearts works against how we were created, and instead moves us toward the will to refuse what we feel, need, desire, long, or hope.

Dissociating (i.e. no longer being associated) from our hearts is unnatural to how we are created, and yet it occurs as a practical and necessary defense. It is understandable to want to protect the heart from more pain than we can bear. However, in squashing our true self through the use of dissociative will power, we become hyper-vigilantly attentive to the environment, as it is now our own authority that tells us who to be. We begin to observe to see what we are supposed to say, instead of having the courage to say what we truly believe or feel. Along with not being able to say what we believe or feel, we also begin to hide the questions of our hearts, the answers to which encourage us to remain true to ourselves.

Holding on to who we are created to be requires that our will be submitted to the heart's voice. Dissociation from our hearts, sadly and understandably, subordinates the heart to willpower.

A GREAT SADNESS

A great sadness is that the heart becomes a rejected treasure a child hides when they do not experience themselves as pursued and affirmed. When the heart is experienced as the enemy of the child, then God, too, can become intuitively and improperly feared or distrusted. That is, approval of God will matter more to the child than the love of God. Rejection by caretakers becomes a rejection of being human, which involves disavowing the emotional and spiritual creature God created. The child intuitively and mistakenly concludes: "How I was created in heart must be a mistake."

Cognitive and defensive structures, sadly, are constructed to distrust, discredit, and avoid the heart. We begin to find our worth in performance or externally-valued behaviors, rather than simply being present with our hearts, others, and God. Religion can be an especially insidious way to hide a relational need of God through performance and behavior, rather than a ritual in which one pours from the fullness of their hearts. As a poor replacement for being fully present with a faithful God, we can start to perform for others and God in an attempt to earn love by "being good" or "doing the right thing." We can begin to perform for God in a way that creates a painful paradox: that which we do to earn the right to express our hearts takes us farther and farther away from how we were created by God.

The truth is that God created us to be present with our hearts, not to perform as a way of gaining the right to become who we are created to be. Remember that both Abraham and Mary responded to God's calling with a simple statement of presence: "Here I am." True performance is to be an expression of presence, not a way to have to earn love or permission to live a life of heart — neither of which can be earned. The great sadness is how far we can remove ourselves from the truth of how we are created.

CAREGIVERS' POWER

Caregivers are profoundly influential in the development of confidence in our relational pre-design and the proper use of willpower. If we are not affirmed and confirmed by caregivers in using the will to openly express feelings, needs, desire, longings, and hope, we understandably develop the willpower to hide our hearts.

One way of hiding, enacted by many children and adults, is to construct a false self that defends against unreceptive or cruel caregivers. They do this by learning to become whoever their caregivers need them to be. Caregivers can either cooperate with creation or attempt to shift creation into something other than what was purposed to grow a certain way.

When caregivers do not cooperate with creation, they, to use a plant metaphor, try to convince the roots of a tree to refrain from water or attempt to make a bloom not face the sun. The beauty of our true selves is that even as the false self covers and protects our hearts, the roots and blooms of who we really are continue to survive through incredible acts of improvisation, while persevering until better conditions come along. For example, the false self protects the child's heart from unsafe people, saving it for people and places who know the heart hungers for relationship with self, others, and God.

Simply put, the child's God-made and even desperate need of affirmation and confirmation from caregivers leads to either expression or suppression of the being God created them to be. If caregivers can affirm and confirm a child's feelings, needs, desire, longings and hope in a good enough way, the child is given a great chance to remain vulnerable enough to continually express their hearts.

HEART'S PRESENCE VS. AVOIDANCE OF HEART

Living our proper craving for life involves the heart seeking gratification, the brain engaging the world, the soul being stilled, and the body becoming directed. The vulnerability of the heart's presence in the midst of craving life puts us in a position to need relationship with God and others.

When we fall into the lust for control, however, the body directs, the brain hunts, the soul wanders, and the heart is temporarily satiated at best. If we do not use the brain to engage the leadership of the heart, the body will take over in our seeking for fulfillment. When we use food, for example, as a cure for a restless heart, we are avoiding the vulnerability of our feelings, needs, desire, longings, and hope. Gorging oneself on carbohydrates for emotional purposes satiates temporarily, as they pass through the blood-brain barrier quickly, temporarily satisfying our need for a sense of well-being. Before long this well-being fades, and even though we just ate, we experience a hunger for the comfort over and over again.

A lust for control is an impaired attempt to find fulfillment without having to fully face the vulnerability of the heart's craving for life. Craving exposes and expresses the need for relationship with others and God in order to experience the life we are created to live.

TRUE NORMAL AND WHAT DISTORTS IT

Our craving for relationship is the true normal of human beings from birth onward. We are often taught, however, that true normal is strange or wrong. After learning this, we become afraid of the vulnerability that comes with being creatures of heart, deciding instead to hide our hearts. In order to get along in life with our hearts hidden away, we are forced into a life of mimicry to fit in. That is, we become mimes performing whatever role seems necessary to gain worth as a person. Under this burden of performance-based personhood, we do whatever seems to sell to our audience or promises to gain us temporary recognition and favor.

For example, when I was a child, I remember my father talking about how pathetic a local teen looked in a pair of bell-bottom jeans. He associated the pants, quite mistakenly, with society's demise. I, on the other hand, saw a cool pair of pants that I wanted. Living in a performance based role, I agreed with my father and said the guy looked stupid or something. I knew that I wasn't telling the truth, but rather the answer my father was looking for. True normal is the ability to identify, explore, and express the heart and the ability to ask for help to do so. It's the way of belonging and mattering as you really are in your heart. Attempting to fit in for the sake of survival makes us common. However, belonging and mattering for who we really are allows us to join with others in relationship — our true normal.

THE MAJORITY OF THE COMMON IS NOT NORMAL

Common is sadly, and often, mistaken for normal. The wide thoroughfare is crowded with the common: people imprisoned by performance-based worth competing for prizes. A less crowded pathway of living is open to the normal: presence-based expression of inherent worth. Although the opening to the pathway is usually opened through the pain of re-association, a pain registered when we feel the impact of having to disassociate, there are many who walk in the way of the normal.

Normal people are accepting of how we are created and who we are created to become. We see who we are made to be so we can do what we are made to do. We live fully, love deeply, lead well as we are directly connected to relationship with ourselves, others, and God.

I will speak of acceptance later, but it means, in short, the courage to keep on living and loving in the face of inevitable loss. Living from the inside-out is not common, but it is normal, and neither are about numbers or majorities—they are simply about either mimicking someone else's life that you cannot have or living into who you are created to become.

CRAVING LIFE FULFILLMENT AND ITS IMPAIRED EXPRESSION, LUST

The head, just like the will, is primarily to be a servant of the heart's craving for life and the heart's image of life fulfilled. The heart's craving for life moves us to live fully.

However, many people have been taught that craving for life, which leads us to step towards our dreams being fulfilled, is somehow wrong. Those who are taught this have confused the heart's craving for life with lust. Craving for life is markedly different than the lust for control. Craving for life remains vulnerable, courageous, and heart-oriented. Living one's craving for life involves a person revealing their hearts to others, expressing full-hearted participation in their dreams (and risking failure to do so), and remaining connected to their own internal images of what could be created for fulfillment.

Lust, on the other hand, is guided by the agenda of avoiding vulnerability, courage, and a heart-orientation. Lust is about control, which is the attempt to negate vulnerability, withhold courage, and hide the heart, while still continuing to seek fulfillment. Lust satisfied satiates, quickly dries up, and intensifies the continuing appetite for more control over people, places, and things. A true craving for life actually gratifies the heart, lasts in memories of gratitude, and inspires us to walk in faith.

RESPONSE-ABILITY VS. REACTIVITY

The heart experiences what I call "response ability" as the true normal at birth. Response-ability is the ability to respond to the heart without defending against its needs or feelings. Response-ability allows our faces and behaviors to match our hearts when we relate to our surroundings, others, and God. In response-ability, the heart of a person is communicated, the face expresses the heart's experience, and the behaviors correspond in an integrated fashion.

When a normal person begins to find their "true normal" responses rejected in their relational surroundings, the heart of the person recoils. Reaction takes the place of response-ability when the heart is rejected. Reactivity is a form of hiding the heart. It is a way of "watching faces," so that we know what to do, how to pretend, or what action to take. Reactivity involves taking actions to control circumstances, instead of being fully present in circumstances.

Reacting to life turns us into common people, so that we can fit into our surroundings for the sake of survival. We develop reactivity at the cost of losing response-ability. We use our faces to hide our hearts in order to stave off further rejection. Tragically, our actions are used to fit in by not being our true selves. In reactivity, the approval of others matters more than knowing ourselves and God.

THE IMPORTANCE OF NOURISHMENT AND EFFECT OF MALNOURISHMENT

Well-nourished roots grow strong. When heat comes, the leaves stay green; when drought comes, the tree bears fruit. In the same way, a well-nourished person draws from relational ties with others and God in the midst of life's difficulties and tragedies.

The essential roots of the heart are feelings, needs, desire, longings and hope. Out of the roots, we connect and imagine, belong and matter, grieve and accept, celebrate and enjoy, intuit and dream. Without these roots being known and nourished, our ability to live well is thwarted, our ability to love is stymied, and our ability to lead others is impaired. We are forced to survive by distrust, becoming hyper-vigilant and defensive, rather than open to the possibility of trusting others. If we do not remain open to receiving nourishment from others and God, we become focused on the preservation of what we have.

A survival focus takes precedence over living openly if a person is not nourished by affirmation and confirmation of their heart's makeup. While a survival focus is understandable, it is ultimately an impaired life of lowered expectations, reduced hope, development of counterfeit fulfillment, and a rejection of our true, relational self.

THE STRUGGLE FOR CONNECTION

The need to belong and the need to matter are the two greatest needs of the human being. These needs are the door to the experience of being fully alive. If the needs to belong and matter are met by the affirmation and confirmation of caregivers, the interplay will strengthen the child's trust and confidence in their heart. This repetitive relational connection fosters hope and faith in children and continues to strengthen grownups in their ability to live fully. Relational connection develops how we are created and who we are created to become.

When caregivers do not generally express affirmation/confirmation of the child's heart, they tend to suppress the heart's inborn desire and the courage to express it in an open and vulnerable way. When the heart is not nourished, the child will move from feeling their way to figuring their way through life. That is, they will place figuring out the world above openly connecting their inner world with the outer world of relationships.

When this happens to us, we figure ways to control the experience of our hearts, rather than use figuring to express the experience of our hearts. In doing so, we develop the defensive ability to hide feelings, deny needs, withhold desire, suppress longings, and diminish hope.

The heart does not go away no matter how it is treated.

It can be imprisoned and diminished or set free and grown. People who develop the trust and confidence in their hearts are able to face their pain, doubt, struggle, grief, joy and hope, allowing them to live a form of freedom that others do not have. This trust and confidence, once again, is birthed and grown through the affirmation and confirmation of the heart in relationship with caregivers initially, and then through trusted others as one grows up.

THE LACK OF AFFIRMATION AND CONFIRMATION

When we are not affirmed and confirmed in heart, we tend to move from our fulfillment-seeking nature at birth to an existence oriented around mere survival. Without receiving affirmation and confirmation for feeling, needing, desiring, longing, and hoping, we must attempt to close off the roots of who we are, as the heart is assumed to be foolish. Naming the heart foolish creates a distance from the heart — a learned distance needed to survive in an malnourishing environment. When we live a life of survival at a distance from the heart, we are forced into attempting to get our emotional and spiritual needs met without the utter vulnerability necessary for the heart's hunger to be satisfied.

Remember, it is integral to the nature of needs that they put us in a position to depend on someone or something outside of ourselves. The life of a survivor is a lonely one that assumes that in order to get love, we must never reveal the neediness of the heart. We attempt to appear stronger, smarter, bigger, and wiser than we really are as a way to "earn" the food of affirmation and confirmation. We hope, in an impaired way, that we can earn love through performing well enough to earn cheers and smiles.

Simply put, we perform instead of remaining present in heart, denying that which leads to vulnerability. Life of heart and vulnerability accepts the truth that we are in desperate need of others and God. Living in heart, however, is impossible without the affirmation and confirmation of others.

THE POTENTIAL LOSS

One way of understanding how a person can develop a way of life based solely on survival is viewing it as a conflict between how we are created and the sickness of the previous generation. If caregivers cannot tolerate having their own hearts disrupted by the pain and struggle of love, the child's heart will be sacrificed to the overt or covert need of caregivers to avoid their own hearts. A child will suppress how they are created to please and avoid caretakers and eventually others. The conflict, then, becomes the struggle between the demand placed on the child by the caretakers to create a false, protective self and the God-given need to live one's true self.

Being forced to develop a false self establishes a trend of hiding our hearts to protect our true selves. The tragedy of protecting ourselves from harm is that a person also loses their ability to allow their hearts to be touched by genuine affirmation and confirmation when it comes to them. The protective shield of distrust and uncertainty protects a person from the dangers of vulnerability, which is the very same vulnerability that allows one to experience the heart being touched. The solution eventually becomes the problem. The problem will affect the next generation. And so it goes, until a return to the heart occurs.

CHAPTER THREE

THE WORK OF HOPE

ooooo

Hope comes with the breath of life. Hope arouses the craving for life and calls us to imagine a future worth having and sharing. The craving for life inspired by hope compels us toward seeking ways to create the future we can imagine. We are called to keep hoping in this manner to our last breath. We are naturally creatures of hope, as we are always moving into the future, desiring it to be a place we can live fully with self, others, and God. Children are born with this hope and the courage to express it. Adults have to fight to hold onto this inborn hope and courage, as we all learn that life on life's terms doesn't always, or even often, look like what we dreamed it could become. Many of us learn to hide our hope after enduring heartache, loss, or pain. We easily drift into merely surviving life. However, even a survival focus is guided by the hope that we can perform well enough or control enough to receive love, freedom, happiness, and safety. Needless to say, it's very difficult to stop imagining a future that either continues our current pleasures or is better than the place in which we are currently. In many ways, we are powerless over hoping. We are given the choice to either surrender to our hope or try to bury it.

HOPE, RISK, AND FAITH

Hope is inherently risky and the paradoxical beginning of faith. The moment we hope, we reach for something we do not have. When our risk of hope is fulfilled, we develop faith. Faith is a belief in the possibility of an imagined future coming true based on past experiences. As Hebrews states, "faith is being sure of what we hope for and certain of what we do not see." Simply, hope, the risk of reaching toward what we can imagine, can result in outcomes that feed our hearts. Hope realized opens us up to celebration and being celebrated by those who love us and supported our hope. Hope and risk also, of course, frustrate or hurt our hearts when life does not go as we imagined. The grief of hopes unattained is to be attended to as completely as the delight of hopes fulfilled. In both cases, faith is being matured, as we are capable of remembering hope being fulfilled and receiving comfort in hope unattained. Both attainment and loss mature faith into a sense of trusting the process of hope and risk, as we come to believe that God is still present no matter the course of our futures.

HOPE AND APATHY

Hope, an inborn quality of the heart, develops its tensile strength in past, present, and future relationships that affirm and confirm the heart. Without the relationships that feed hope, its continuous deferment starves the heart, though hope remains. Hope deferred over and over, can lead to a contempt for hope. Hope rejected and despised can lead to hope's antithesis: apathy. Apathy is the most tragic and near complete loss of the self, for apathy says, "I refuse to dream about the future. I don't care what happens." Apathy is the refusal to attach, to care, to love, to long, to desire, and to hope. This apathy towards hope, toward its rumblings within us, makes us give little value to our own hearts and those of others. Apathy is what allows evil to be birthed and to flourish.

HOPE'S DARING

The ever present temptation toward apathy is the reason hope is daring and so risky. Hope awakens us to wonder, wishes, dreams, courage, and belief. These forms of imagining will always be slightly painful when we discover that we live east of Eden and west of glory. After experiencing this pain, hope must be sustained and nourished by others and God. This relational sustenance allows us to persevere in all such imaginings, giving us the courage that can only come with being known in heart. The moment we hope, we picture something we long for and desire, something that has not yet happened. These longings and pictures of desire bring with them exhilaration and fear. This exhilaration comes from the excitement of anticipation, while the fear comes from the knowledge that not all wishes are fulfilled. We really do dare to hope, dare to face the very thing within us that comes with us at birth.

HOPE, FEAR, AND TRUST

In hope, we seek what we do not yet have. This seeking of what is only imagined brings with it the fear that we may not reach our dreams, that it will be a hard journey in trying, and so on. As we are creatures born with hope in our hearts, we are clearly intended to become very good at feeling fear, as hope and fear work together. Hope plus risk/reaching (fear), can allow us to experience an outcome favorable to what we seek. Hope can even allow us to risk again after disappointment, even as we learn more about the effects of risk/reaching. Even if failure occurs, we hope, because we are made to seek living fully, loving deeply, and leading well. An outcome that is favorable to what we hoped creates a memory of how hope and fear can turn out well, building a stronger and stronger sense of trust in life, others, the process of living, and God. The memory of life working in relationship with ourselves, others, and God eventually becomes an experiential knowledge of how to live in hope. The development of trusting hope and learning how to trust and use fear well occurs over time, as we become capable of tolerating outcomes that don't fit with our hope and continue to hope anyway.

CHAPTER FOUR

LESSONS FROM LONGING

∞∞∞

LONGINGS

Longings come to us as real as breath. We cannot escape them, though we can spend our lives running from them. Longings reveal how far away we live from that which we most hope could be true. While longings disclose how far from Home we truly are, they also move us to create that which matters to us despite knowing that our lives will never be perfect or complete. Longings call us into the struggle to make life better than it will ever become. We are called to fully participate in the beautiful failure of living. Longings teach us how to live fully in a place of impermanence and incompletion. The inevitable incompletion of life undoubtedly has a trace of the tragic to it. In order for longings to lead us to living well, however, this sense of tragedy must be held in tension with the belief that God is faithful amidst the tragic. Life is tragic; God is faithful. Longings point to this reality and truth. They speak to that which hope most hopes: a home that is always permanent, a peace that is secure and never changes, a justice that is certain and lasts, and a safety that is guaranteed.

> We long for a home we never have to leave or
> struggle in.
> We long for a peace that does not become disrupted.
> We long for a justice that protects us all from harm.
> We long for a safety that is not up to us in a world
> that is never, ever, ever going to be what we can
> imagine.

LONGINGS LIVED IN THIS LIFE

We can experience, in incomplete ways, what longings call us toward. The more we allow ourselves to long, the greater our pain will be. Our pain increases with longing, because we see more fully the distance between what our hearts can envision and the reality of what often occurs. This gap is the reason longings call us to feel all of our feelings, as all of our feelings will be needed to hope, long, reach, build, and not completely succeed. Longings call us to a loneliness that does not end, a sadness that will not stop, a hurt that cannot be healed, an anger that cannot be resolved, a fear that cannot be helped, and a neediness that brings us closer to God and others than we would have ever been otherwise. Very courageous people build in a world that will be torn down. Despite the inherent pain, the longing heart also has the gratitude of a direction to follow, a mission to pursue, a faith to walk in, and a promise to keep. People open to deep longings live as they are created to live in a place that is not completely home, and often not peaceful, just, or safe.

LIVING LONGINGS DAILY

Longings draw their energy from the desire, needs, and feelings we were born to express as emotional and spiritual creatures. As longings come from an eternal place we can only sense, we will become more exhausted the farther we move towards building the impossible on earth. This tension we live in between here and eternity requires that we develop the ability to live in a dependence on the God of the process to handle the future we move towards that will always remain incomplete. As strange as it may seem when discussing longings, the present is where we can live daily with an impact as we build with an eye on a horizon. Daily life is a gift that must not be looked over while gazing toward the horizon. We must live the day we have, then replenish and recreate for tomorrow, to live the next day. One day at a time. If we try to live more than one day at a time, while focused on the future, we will burn up, burn out, give up, quit, and sink in despair. Daily life is where we truly experience emotionally and spiritually the bumps and bruises, the exhilarations and ecstasies of joy of living. Longings are not our escape from the present, but more a point on the horizon we are always moving towards. The horizon created by longings suffuses our daily lives with the magic of dreams, hopes, and wishes. We will forever be called to live in two places at once: the earth and eternity.

What a hard reality: to be born for fulfillment in a place that cannot complete us, yet it can bring us inspiration and great joy if lived emotionally and spiritually.

CHAPTER FIVE

RECOGNIZING YOUR DESIRE

ooooo

DESIRE

Desire exists at the nexus between biology and spirituality. In its purest form, desire is no more than a rudimentary physiological hunger to live fully. Everything that is alive seeks life. The energy of desire pushes us toward needing and feeling, longing and hoping. We are born with desire, just as we are born with hope, longings, needs, and feelings. Desire moves us to participate in a world that can frustrate us and bring us immense pleasure. While longings move us toward a spiritual life, desire is the energy, pulse, and backbeat of all animate life seeking its own fulfillment. If not recognized for what it is, desire can be a cause of great harm to self and others. This is because desire is a force that simply seeks life, no matter what it costs others. Without the development of empathy, being able to emotionally and spiritually identify with others, desire can become a detriment to finding relational fulfillment in a productive way. Desire to live that denies the emotional and spiritual makeup of human beings creates a disconnect from relational life. Desire that disconnects from relationship devolves into a life that merely feeds biology rather than the emotional and spiritual makeup of the heart.

DEVELOPED DESIRE

Through the development of empathy, we are able to connect to the true heart of the human being and live lives of emotional and spiritual fulfillment. In emotionally and spiritually developed grownups, desire moves us to actively participate in what we are created to do. Developed desire leads us to live lives of passion, intimacy, and integrity regardless of what we do for a living. Irrespective of what our desire specifically translates into as we grow into who we are created to become, desire has some specific ends to be directed towards so that we can live fully, love deeply, and lead well. Some of the specific ends of desire are to desire and live whatever is true, noble, right, pure, lovely, admirable, excellent, or praiseworthy. A grownup's heart is fully in the process of living out of the heart, and living in such desire.

AN EXCELLENT WAY

An excellent way to live is with passion, intimacy, and integrity. Excellent is not a form of perfection. Excellent, or to excel, means a reduction of friction in a world that will always create friction. Passion is a willingness to be in pain for something that matters more than pain. It moves a person to give their heart over to something greater than one's own comfort or control. Intimacy is the openness to allow someone to "into-me-see." A heart open to being known is a heart open to living relationally and fully. Integrity is the congruence of the inner life and the outer expression, making one worthy of being trusted.

IMPAIRED DESIRE

Desire is greater than one's own control. It may be more correct, in fact, to say that desire lives us. Simply, we are excessive creatures. If we do not face the power of our desire, feel it, and surrender to the process of its development in us, we will become obsessed with controlling it and the environment it inhabits. The truth is that our hearts will always crave more and imagine more than what we are capable of accomplishing and doing on this earth. This very excessiveness will take the form of lust if we are unable to surrender to the truth, even grievous truth, that we can never be completely fulfilled here. Desire converted into lust enslaves us to mere biology. Lust demands that we grasp at forms of control that minimize the vulnerability and pain of desire. It is a form rejecting neediness, trust, and having to wait. In lust, we attempt to control the world so that we will never have to feel the pain of ungratified desire. In short, we try to turn the earth into heaven. Developed desire, on the other hand, surrenders to the truth of our desire, rather than trying to frantically make sure we will get exactly what we want. While lust eventually becomes the will to suppress the heart's open participation in life, developed desire becomes the courage to live a life of full-hearted participation, in spite of the struggle that opens us to vulnerability and pain. There is not enough money, sex, safety, travel, exercise, thought, philosophy, religion, or drugs to take us away from how we are created. We either surrender to how we are created, or we will use our will power to attempt to escape the necessary surrender to and development of desire.

CHAPTER SIX

NEEDS ARE NOT LUXURIES

ooooo

NEEDS

Needs connect us all together. The most basic truth about needs cannot be repeated frequently enough: needs are not luxuries. They are integral to the formation of human connection and fulfillment. Needs actually allow us to live fully in relationship with ourselves, others and God. Needs bring us into relationship with ourselves as we face our neediness. Once we wake up to our own neediness, we are compelled to find others who have done the same, those who have faced how they are made. Finally, our neediness brings us into relationship with the God who created us. In a strange way, needs "force" us into relationship. Getting our needs addressed is essential to living, and we cannot meet the needs of how we are created without relationship with others and God. We either have them met openly and truthfully, or through some form of manipulation.

BELONGING, MATTERING, AND GROWTH

The two most powerful needs of the human heart are to belong and to matter. Getting these needs met is a deeply important task, as vital as food, water, shelter and clothing. If we are not fed the food of relationship that meets the needs to belong and to matter, we move towards a survival focus. Characteristics displayed by those in survival mode often include a range of symptoms to take one away from the pain of the heart: practicing forms of hopelessness, lowering expectations, becoming ashamed of one's internal makeup, focusing on relief, and seeking counterfeit fulfillments for relational needs. On the other hand, a life full of emotional and spiritual relationship allows one to live life with abandon. Simply, the power of knowing that we belong and matter sets one free to live life with full-hearted participation. The need to belong is fulfilled through being affirmed as acceptable and normal as an emotional and spiritual creature. Mattering is fulfilled by being confirmed in one's unique, individual giftedness in the life of a community. All other human needs grow out of and work in accordance with the two primary needs. A common characteristic of all needs is that they function to fulfill us emotionally and spiritually. And the experience of fulfillment always occurs through relationship.

THE MATURE NEED BEST

Being able to need well is the primary marker of being a grownup. Other markers are the capacity to feel, desire, long and hope. Sadly, many people become adults instead of growing up, and childhood is often associated with a condition that we move out of rather than continue to grow up from. Growing up is much like the way trees grow by adding concentric circles, with the rings of life marking the growth around the heart of the tree. The rings extend from the essential nature of the tree and are expressions of the tree's root system being fed. A well-fed tree matures out of the core by expanding through proper nurturance. Much like tree growth, a person who is fed emotional and spiritual food as a child grows up with the ability to "keep heart." On the other hand, when a person works against the God created process of growth from the heart outward, the results can be tragic. For example, many people are ashamed of their need for attention. Attention means to be tended to or nurtured, which is a need that can only be met through confession to trusted others and God. Simply, we can only be attended to if others know we need attention. People who serve others, in particular, need a great deal of attention. Many of these servants unfortunately deny their need for attention, because they are ashamed of their own neediness. Those of us who are ashamed of our neediness have become adults, rather than remaining committed to growing up via getting our emotional and spiritual needs met by others and God. Grownups and adults differ in that the grownup faces the vulnerability of need and expresses it, while the adult has contempt and shame regarding their needs.

NEEDS: Our needs are primarily relational, and, therefore, cannot not be legitimately met except in relationship with our selves, others, and God.

> ATTENTION: to be nurtured or tended to.
> GRIEF: allowing our selves to experience the sadness of a life that is full of loss.
> ACCOMPLISHMENT: identifying when to stop, celebrate, and rest.
> TOUCH: to experience that which gratifies the heart.
> SECURITY: knowing that my vulnerability is acceptable and significant
> SEXUALITY: having comfort and confidence in my own skin as male or female.
> GUIDANCE: receiving help to discover where I need to go.
> SUPPORT: encouragement to move towards where one cannot go alone, but must do what needs to be done.
> TRUST: being able to rely on another's dependability.

LISTENING: to experience oneself as known and seen
by another and the ability to do the same.

FREEDOM: living fully and response-ably

FUN: the full engagement of a person in whatever they
have given themselves to.

CHAPTER SEVEN

I FEEL; THEREFORE, I AM

ooooo

FEELINGS

Feelings bring us into a connective, experiential relationship with our outer worlds and ourselves. Feelings influence our behaviors and thoughts, inform our desire, and help us process longings and hope. Their interplay with the world helps us feel fully alive. *Sentio ergo sum* — I feel; therefore I am — is a core truth about human beings, allowing us to know and trust where we are in this life. Keeping heart, which begins with feelings, separates those who live fully through full-hearted participation from those who are sleepwalkers in life, waiting at a depot where the train never comes.

THE CORE FEELINGS

We have been given eight core feelings, or eight tools, that allow us to live fully in a tragic place — a place in which things we don't want to occur can and do occur. The desperation of hope and the courage to express it shows how amazing we are. We keep on living in spite of difficulties that complicate all of life. We seek life in spite of all the death, despair, destruction, and darkness. Feelings give us a response ability to struggle for life, and feelings allow us to take responsibility for our lives.

While there are only eight feelings, this number is not limiting. Quite the converse, actually. Feelings allow us to deal with limits, to experience life on its own terms, and work towards the lives we wish to have. Moreover, they are not negative. What we DO behaviorally with our feelings can stymie our fulfillment and create great loss, however. At some point in our lives, many of us learned to use behaviors to react to our feelings, rather than to respond to our feelings relationally. If not encouraged to experience and share feelings, we develop contempt for or practice ignoring how we are created as feeling creatures. This potential reactive point is where our problems begin and continue if we do not recover the ability to be vulnerable enough to listen to the voice of our hearts. Feelings are a gift of creation.

The core feelings are:

SADNESS

ANGER

HURT

FEAR

LONELINESS

SHAME

GUILT

GLADNESS

CORE FEELINGS, PRIMARY COLORS, AND MUSICAL NOTES

The core feelings are like the three primary colors. With the palette of the three primary colors, artists create endless shades and tones of expression. With three primary colors, we find the fuller expression of all color. For example, there are approximately fifty-two shades of green in Ireland alone. There are also a certain number of musical notes. A person who can use the notes takes what seems like a limitation and integrates them into an infinite number of compositions. A composer can never get to the end of the possibilities offered by a limited amount of notes. Life's givens are the paradoxical doorway to infinite possibilities. Feelings can be compared to primary colors and musical notes in that there are a limited number of tools that allow humans to express and create infinite varieties of life. They set us free to respond to life on life's terms — its losses and its wonders. Feelings are creations' tools that allow us to live fully, love deeply, and lead well. Feelings are good, and each feeling delivers gifts, just as using the primary colors yields to the artist's brush and musical notes express the composer's imagination.

FEELINGS AS ENERGY

Feelings are a type of energy in motion — e-motion — that is made to move us toward wholeness and presence. Many people struggle mightily against the energy of feelings. These people are in conflict with their own hearts, and cannot become whole or fully present as long as they work against the expression of feelings. These people have forgotten the colors and notes that allow us to express life and live fully in it. Working against the expression and experience of feelings often begins with wounds or parental practices, both of which create distrust, denial, and dissociation from the heart. The will to control the energy generated by feelings works against the healthy expression of feelings. A healthy human being has their voice working in congruence with the rumblings of the heart.

EXPLORING THE HEART: FEELINGS AS PASSWORDS, LANTERNS, AND KEYS

Upon the doorway of the human heart are written the eight core feelings. We cannot enter the doorway of our own hearts unless we use the language the heart speaks, and the heart demands that we learn its language, not the other way around. In exploring the terrain of the heart, the eight core feelings operate first as passwords that let us both enter our own hearts and let our hearts speak to ourselves, others, and God. After gaining entrance into the heart, feelings function as lanterns that allow us to explore our hearts after we enter. They shine on the inner rooms of the self and highlight our needs, desire, longings, and hope. For example, I might feel afraid and see that I need security, desire help, long for a life that isn't so frightening, and hope that I will be "ok" in spite of how scary life is. The lantern of feelings sheds light on the need, the desire, the longing, and the hope. Finally, feelings work as keys. They open rooms within us that are meant to be explored and aired out with safe people and God. Entering the rooms of the heart expands the life we live, allowing our worlds to be more open, as we no longer fear what we may find in our hearts. Feelings open doors to let others live life with us, letting us know them and love them more deeply.

THE SPIRITUAL ROOT SYSTEM™

Feelings Hope

Needs Longings

Desire

Order exists within us. We are created a specific way. The eight feelings begin the life of response and connection between our hearts and the world. Feelings awaken us to needs that can be communicated to our selves, others, and God, if we remain sensitive to voicing what happens within us. Needs point towards our desire for life itself. Desire speaks towards the longings to have life a certain way. And longings bring us to envisioning and working toward a life we hope for. This hope returns us to the necessity of our feelings, for with every hope we have feelings. Experiencing our feelings, needs, desire, longings, and hope, moreover, is the precursor to the human imagination, the ability to envision and create. The heart permitted its expression can see worlds not created. The Spiritual Root System™ opens us up to imagine fulfillment and freedom, while also allowing us to grieve how far we are from our internal, imagined destination, if we will but continue to listen to and express our hearts.

OUR ORIGINAL PICTURE

One of the first applications of our hearts to life and first examples of how incipient intellect, willpower, and morality submit to the heart is the inborn desire for attachment to our caregivers. Our first image of fulfillment and completion, done intuitively, is reaching for the caregiver who will live fully with us, love us deeply, and lead us well. If we are fortunate enough to connect to caregivers who know that intellect, will power, and morality are functions that are to be submitted to the heart's primacy, we tend to live fully or keep heart as a way of life. In other words, our connection to trusted caregivers does, indeed, guide us as to how we live in a tragic world in which God is faithful.

EUPHORIA RIVER

Life is lived on a continuum between the gifts of celebration and grief. The space between these two polarities is called "Euphoria River." Euphoria means to bear well, and we are created to bear life well. Euphoria River is where we live the process of all that life has to offer, which is done by feeling our feelings, telling the truth of our hearts, and giving ourselves to the process of living how we are created to live. On Euphoria River, we experience and express hope and sadness, joy and loss, hurt, anger, needs, wishes, yearnings, disappointments, periods of great struggle, and periods of sweet ease. It takes a lot of heart, a bunch of trusted others, and an intimacy with God to live life on life's terms with a wide open heart. Only through relational connection with others and God, are we able to live fully between loss and wonder, grief and celebration.

PARTICIPATION IN LOVE

We contend with the difficulties of life, even the tragedy of life, by participating in love. Through love we bring light into darkness, creation into destruction, hope into despair, and courage into death. The tools of the heart offer us a capacity to fight well as people who believe in more than just survival. We who are fully alive carry within us a desire born of empathy to participate in making life on earth better. Participating in love is not always dramatic or epic, though it can be. Those of us who participate in love move into territories of poverty, injustice, starvation, cruelty, and indignity that mar our lives and others. We raise families, participate in society, meet needs. We raise vegetables, plant flowers, pick up trash. We participate in a multitude of ways in the world around us, from career paths to sharing lunch with someone. This participation in love is to be lived in our daily lives, in the comings and goings of our daily rhythms. We must have the tools of the heart, live in relationship, and allow ourselves to live on Euphoria River to live such a life.

- SAD -

Sadness is the attachment feeling. When we lose someone, someplace, or something that matters to our hearts, we feel sad. Sadness occurs as a result of caring. Without the willingness to experience sadness, we defend against letting ourselves care. Even when something great and wonderful comes to a beautiful close, the heart has sadness. The experience of sadness allows us to move into the gift of acceptance. Acceptance does not occur as a decision (intellect), force (will power) or "should-ism" (morality). Acceptance is a matter of the heart. Acceptance does not mean "It's OK," as it is so often said. Acceptance means "It is not OK, and that is OK." In other words, acceptance allows us to continue to be sad that loss has occurred, while also freeing us to attach anew. Acceptance allows us to keep courage in the face of inevitable loss. Through our willingness to feel and trust the process, we are resolved to care and attach in a world in which loss comes with all love. In sum, acceptance is the willingness to care and move forward again in the face of inevitable loss. Sometimes, acceptance takes a long time to come to us. However, it never leaves "It's not OK" behind, because we know in our hearts that life is made to be better than it so often occurs.

SAD: SADNESS AND HONOR

Sadness honors the loss that comes with change. In a world where change and loss are inevitable, the willingness to have sadness allows us to remain fully alive. A stoic approach assumes that feeling sadness or continuing to care and attach in a world of inevitable loss is illogical. Why care about people, places, and things that we will lose, and the loss of which will cause us pain? When a person becomes terminally hard or calloused against sadness through logic, drugs, sex, and so on, they lose the capacity to attach, care, and participate in life. This person loses more when they intend never to lose again. A person becomes impaired when they are in denial, blind, or ignore their own make-up as a result of trauma or otherwise. The good news, however, is that we do not have to be destroyed by loss. We can keep caring. Those people who do not become calloused, honor loss with their sadness, and they become prepared over time to care again.

SAD: IMPAIRED SADNESS

Self-pity is impaired sadness. Calling impaired sadness self-pity is neither a judgment, nor a statement of badness, however. Self-pity is a willful attempt to escape sadness through judging one's self as defective, doomed, or believing one has rights on life that others' don't have, e.g., "this event should never happen to me." Self-pity is a result of having an intolerance for sadness. In fact, people who become stuck in self-pity are actually afraid to grieve because of shame, ignorance, denial, or trauma. Essentially, they have loved and lost, and on some level are committed to never lose again. Self-pity blocks us from risking attachment again, because it will inevitably lead to the losses that come with letting one's self care deeply. A person in self-pity demands that others do the sadness work for them. That person doesn't yet have the heart or courage to be sad. Again, self-pity is not bad. It is, nevertheless, a form of what happens when we are in conflict with our own makeup. It is an attempt to avoid facing and feeling life on life's terms and seeking a God that seems very far away.

SAD: THE GIFT OF ACCEPTANCE

Acceptance, which develops out of true sadness, enriches us. The courage to have sadness sheds light on the pathway of living fully, loving deeply, and leading well. No one else can live our lives for us. We are the ones who must risk. The choice: to care, attach, have poetry and heartache, grandeur and wonder, memories, struggle and tragedy in our quest of living, or remove ourselves from care and drift in a sea of isolation that protects us from how we are made to care.

- ANGER -

Anger is the most vulnerable feeling of all the feelings. It reveals what we care most about, that which matters to us. Anger expresses a reaching towards something, our hearts' desire for change and creativity. It exposes us as vulnerable and dependent. Contrary to popular opinion, anger does not harm, yet is willing to be hurt. What is often called anger is actually shear rage, which is the opposite of anger. Rage destroys everything in its path in an attempt to remain invulnerable, as rage feels powerful. It will murder to keep from being exposed as dependent and vulnerable, while anger will die for something worth fighting for. Rage is ruled by terror; anger is guided by God-given desire. The feeling of anger grows into many other words that we know: hoping, wishing, yearning, longing, wanting, desiring, hungering, thirsting, wondering, imagining, caring, and willing. All of these words require the anger that compels us to reach towards someone, something, or someplace. The list of words that describe anger are usually associated with weakness, as they admit one's lack of self-sufficiency; yet, they are expressions of wanting life. They reveal truths about one's self, and hide nothing. Anger reveals the capacity for full presence and full participation.

ANGER: ORIGIN OF RAGE

If we cannot handle the fear that comes from hoping and caring, that fear of failure or helplessness becomes terror. If we are then rendered helpless, rage often results. Rage expresses contempt toward our humanity in a self-protective, yet tragically self-destructive dynamic. Rage suppresses vulnerability and allows potential helplessness to have sway. Rage attempts to protect against helplessness at any costs; therefore, in the name of self-protection, one will destroy whatever is threatening. Because much of our helplessness is related to experiences of our vulnerability being rejected by people we care about, rage is often played out against people the one who rages cares about. No one else can trigger helplessness, the powerful threat of abject abandonment to aloneness, as much as a someone we care about, in addition to conditions that are pointed reminders of our past helplessness.

ANGER: THE BEAUTY OF ANGER

Anger creates, reaches out, and perseveres in pain for a purpose. Love moves in anger. True mothers, fathers, children, composers, generals, scientists, and creators have anger —the courage of hope and the willingness to express it. Our anger grows us into passionate people who are willing to be in pain for something greater than the pain. Hope is the most passionate expression of anger, as it is the essential desire for life that moves us to plant seeds, tend to growth, and anticipate a harvest. When anger is denied or ignored, the one's life desire is depressed, making it null. The action of depressing one's desire is like putting a rock on a seed. It doesn't stop how the seed is made to rise and grow; it does, however, suppress the expression of life.

ANGER: THE GIFT OF PASSION

Passion is the gift of letting ourselves grow in anger. Passion blesses us by giving us more of life in life. Passion animates the world, making colors shine brighter, sounds ring clearer, and our hearts yearn fiercely. It is a willingness to be in pain for something that matters more than pain. No anger, no passion. No passion, no creation. No creation, no energy of participation in the fight for love. The choice: to risk desire and know what matters to you as you submit to the hero or heroine's quest for life. Or depress the desire for life, and eat the dust of rejecting life's dynamism.

- HURT AND RESENTMENT -

Hurt can move us toward our need for healing and the decision to live in courage as we return to life in healing. Healing occurs in many forms, but there is an "re" in all healing. As we participate in the struggle of daily life, we experience bruises, some worse than others. Each day needs to end in a "re" of healing. We re-turn, re-store, re-plenish, re-create, re-cover, re-pent, and re-st. If we do not attend to the wounds of living, we have a tendency to become resentful. Attempting to keep our selves from ever getting hurt puts us in a position of defensiveness, i.e., when we are threatened by hurt or experience hurt, we find someone to blame, judge or reject. This cycle of resentment is a way to never have to admit hurt, which is done by blaming others or life for always hurting us. Admitting hurt leaves us vulnerable and in need of healing. Resentment can become an impaired stance of approaching life. It demands that life or the other change before we significantly engage with our hearts. Only healing from hurt allows us to reengage with life.

HURT: COURAGE AS RELATED TO HURT

Hurt and courage work together. After a person is hurt emotionally, or even physically, they are more fully aware of the costs of participating in life. There is tremendous learning that occurs in the process of healing. Out of this process grows a knowledge of solutions to pain, a more experienced understanding about how to live and operate in the midst of hurt, and a greater capacity to decide how we will participate in life and with whom. Acknowledging and processing hurt brings us to pain we likely never wished for, yet the process of healing yields inevitable benefits. For one, the healing process requires and develops courage. A healing/healed person persisted in seeking solutions and participation in life, rather than devolving into mere survival. By keeping heart, they returned to living fully. Daily life itself requires that we be prepared for hurt, and have the courage to be able to deal with it for our ongoing benefit. Fully participating in life means that we will have all the experiences that come with living fully. If we live with courage, we will get hurt and must heal to be able to live again. Hurt tells us that we have experienced a wound, and we can keep on participating if we receive the help of healing that can return us to living well.

HURT: THE IMPORTANCE OF "RE"

Because daily life itself will present us with inevitable wounds, we need to recognize that daily life requires daily "re" experiences. Every day in which we give our hearts to living means that there is an emptying, like a pitcher that was full of water in the morning and is poured out by the end of an event. The pitcher needs to be refilled to be more than an empty vessel. We need to participate in the experiences of "re" to continue to be able to fully participate in the lives we are capable of living. Daily replenishment, restoration, recovery, redemption, relaxing, and recreation are forms of repairing ourselves to live the next day well. There are many more "re" experiences and each one has its own distinct gift. They are required for us to be able to fully participate in the passions, purposes, and plans that we have for living.

HURT: LOVE, HELP, AND HELPERS

Some of our worst wounds occur in love. No one will ever love without hurt, which is what makes love require so much faith and hope. Words hurt us terribly, especially from those people we care most about. Hurt tells us we have a wound, and that we need to stop and receive healing as soon as we are able to do so. We heal by facing our wounds, feeling them, and turning them over to the process. We need those who know how to care for pain to surround us during times of healing. The helpers/healers do not take us away from our hearts and our desire to live fully, love deeply and lead well. They help return us, replenish us to life, or help recognize our hurts for the sake of healing. Hurt people who lean into healing eventually become people who help others who are hurt. Hurt people who don't do so, hurt others.

- FEAR -

Contrary to what is so often assumed, fear is not an emotion that creates avoidance and withdrawal. It does not stop us from fully participating in our lives and the events within them by any means. For example, I never wish to fly with a fearless pilot, one who does not follow a checklist, while preparing to succeed in his or her mission. Fear allows us to prepare before we move, knowing what possibilities or dangers exist. It leads to a wisdom that acknowledges the dangers of living, while maintaining an ability to live fully despite the inherent perils. Simply, fear makes us aware that we can be negatively affected. If we will deal with fear truthfully, it can help us identify what we value and prepare us to take thoughtful action. Fear aids us in the process of living well by spurring us to action based on who and what we love and desire. Moreover, it prepares us to take action by letting us know that danger is possible, prompting us to seek help. It moves us to cry out for help and seek guidance. Fear can help us become wise when facing the risks that come with how we are created, allowing us to live fully, love deeply, and lead well.

FEAR: FEAR AND ANGER

We are not to use fear as a tool to stop living our lives. On the contrary, fear is created to prepare for living lives that are often scary. Fear prepares us to live fully, love deeply, and lead well, knowing that with our risk of living comes sadness, anger, hurt, more fear, and loneliness, healthy shame, guilt, and gladness. The beauty of the feelings is that they are created to work in concert with one another. If all we could feel, for example, was fear, we would never move. This is why it is important to surrender to feeling all of our feelings fully, as this action allows us to engage with life in profound ways. Thankfully, anger works well in relationship with fear. Anger allows us to take action in spite of the knowledge that events could turn out poorly or not go as we dreamed. Fear prepares us for the unknown future that anger hurls us into. Said another way, fear prepares to offer ourselves fully to living and loving by telling us of the past and potential darkness, destruction, despair, and death we may encounter or have encountered. Anger, as fear's necessary companion, allows us to bring light, creation, hope, and courage into the places our fear has found.

FEAR: FEAR AND THE UNKNOWN

We do not truly fear the unknown. In reality, we fear a recurrence of painful events that we have already experienced, seen, or know have happened to someone else. This fear of recurrence is both understandable and works to trap us in a vicious cycle. When we get stuck in allowing past pains, either that we have experienced ourselves or others we know have experienced, to dictate future risks, then we are in danger of coloring our futures with the pains of the past. We color our futures with past pains in order to make them more predictable, which we think leads to less pain. Hoping for a future that is different than the past becomes tantalizing, as the hope for positive change becomes as or more frightening than the past we have already endured. Outcomes that are better than the past become as anxiety provoking as the past itself.

Ironically, the safest place we know is the strange comfort of knowing bad things will happen and always remaining prepared for them through anxiety and its subsequent control factors. Our safety becomes our vigilant preparation for a repetition of the past. This dynamic is what we have for so long called fear of the unknown when it is actually the fear of our past pains, many of which have never been processed or dealt with emotionally. If our pasts dictate the future and our ability to hope for life to be different/better than our pasts, then we cannot go into tomorrow unless we keep it in the comfort zone of yesterday. We don't have control over much of what tomorrow will bring, but if we have experience in the process and growing trust in our ability to live in it, we can walk through our fears into the mystery of life unfolding into its possibilities, rather than being determined by the losses that have already occurred. We understandably fear the history of our yesterdays. And yet we are created for the mysteries of our tomorrows.

FEAR: ANXIETY AS FEAR GONE AWRY

Anxiety expresses an impairment of healthy fear. It attempts to control what we cannot control — LIFE. Anxiety often operates by trying to keep our lives so small and our field of mastery so large that our worlds are completely predictable, safe, stable, and purposively boring. Anxiety operates to prevent something dreaded from occurring, and there are many things for humans to dread. These goals, while not bad in themselves, squash the craving for a life of passion and vision that we are created to live, as these emotional and spiritual experiences thrive in the unknown and unpredictable world of life on life's terms.

While anxiety is certainly physiological in nature, as it arouses hyper-vigilance in the brain, it also subordinates the heart of hope and imaginative desire to a survival mechanism. The heart will give its life to that which matters more than survival, while a life lived solely under the aegis of anxiety will not. The reality of living with anxiety is not a judgment upon ourselves as failed. It is just the way we operate. Humans will never live without anxiety, as it is not possible to perfectly process fear at all moments. The difference between a life dominated by anxiety and one in which fear is processed, however, is that a person living under the domination of anxiety doesn't ask for help and remains alone. Anxiety attempts to control our lives in order to avoid the vulnerability that being helped entails. Fear, on the other hand, calls out for help, allowing us to speak what we fear and receive the help we need to wisely handle the fear.

FEAR: ANXIETY IN CONFLICT WITH THE CRAVING FOR RELATIONSHIP

Anxiety unintentionally, and often unconsciously, fights against love and genuine relationship. This is the case because anxiety usually begins with a breakdown in love that leaves the heart unattended. During these breakdowns, we are left helpless over getting the nourishment of love our hearts desperately need. The resulting anxiety triggers a person to try to get control of people, places, and things in an attempt to stop utter helplessness from occurring again. We try to cover the terror of not being attended to with anxiety, which will often take the place of crying out for relationship. The painful paradox in all this is that the heart needs to cry out for relationship, yet it's this very same crying out that harmed us in the first place when it was not attended to. When we try to stop the heart from its God-made hope and courage, we inevitably increase our pain, as the anxiety that comes from not seeking relationship with others and God blocks us from the help we actually need. Simply, anxiety strives for control, while the heart craves relationship.

Genuine relationship, which the heart is created to experience, reawakens and revitalizes the heart. Healthy relationships greatly reduce anxiety and can help return it to its proper place as the brain's emergency anticipatory warning system. Relationship is what allows us to receive the help we need. It allows us to risk hoping that our need for help will be met by others and God, moving us to use vulnerability as a form of trust and courage. Anxiety tells us that we can prevent helplessness from recurring by controlling or limiting the impact of our environment. Fear, as a feeling that leads us to our need for relationship, asks us to address what we need and who we need as we interact with the warp and woof of our environments. Fear moves us to get help, risk accepting help, and trust the help provided by others and God. Those of us who are stymied by anxiety spend much of our lives attempting to stop what has already occurred, while we miss the help that we can receive in genuine relationship.

FEAR: ANXIETY, RAGE, AND LOVE

Anxious people who cannot get enough control eventually take flight into rage. Whether it is silent or loud, reclusive or outspoken, rage destroys in its attempts to stop the relational neediness of fear. Rage has no open hand and holds no one's hand. Anxious people control and rage. This dynamic pushes other people away, as we are not created to be controlled by someone's rage or to find our lives in their terror. Unacknowledged anxiety stymies our lives to the point that its overwhelming sirens eventually control the dance of life in relationship with our selves, others, and God. People who face their fears as their own and work with their fears become generative people of faith and wisdom. Our fear of rejection is our greatest fear, which makes love our most feared possibility. We must face and feel our fear to have lives of love. The choice: To develop faith in following our hope for belonging and mattering, or to grasp at control in an attempt to stop all pain, which means having no life.

- LONELY -

Loneliness speaks to how we are made for relationship. It tells us how incomplete we are without each other. It speaks to the blessing and pain of sincere connection. We are lonely for time and space with ourselves to rest, restore, create, imagine, meditate, pray, and move about. We are lonely for those who we can see into and they into us. Loneliness brings us to the experience of intimacy — "into-me-see." Intimacy is birthed in the gift of the feeling of loneliness. Good things in this life occur when one is known from the inside out. We are also lonely for God's Presence in our lives, to experience the touch of relationship with God. We are created by God to have a relational experience of God and the life God has created. Good things happen in people's lives who have intimacy with God and all God has created.

LONELY: LONELINESS AND ITS CALL TO FOUR RELATIONSHIPS

Loneliness calls us to multiple vulnerabilities. We are made incomplete, making us vulnerable, in need. It is the way we learn to use our incompletion that determines how we experience it. In other words, incompletion can be experienced as terrifying, as a wound, or it can lead us to seek relationship. The vulnerabilities of loneliness invite us to speak out of the heart to express our need for a bond with our own inner beings, with others, and with God.

After loneliness awakens us to our need for relationship with our own hearts, others' hearts and the heart of God, we enter a fourth loneliness. While it may seem strange at first, we experience a loneliness to have a relationship with the earth, making from it that which benefits, blesses, and bestows favor upon ourselves, others, and God. We are lonely to make something of great value through putting our imaginations, dreams, and goals into action. Creating out of our imaginations gratifies the heart deeply, as it allows us to bless the earth and for creation, in turn, to bless us. When we see an ancient cathedral, a mother's caress of a child, a hand reaching to help another arise, bread sliced to share, or a feat of magnitude completed, we affirm the glory of this life. Creation becomes more alive to us in our own creative actions. If we face and feel our loneliness courageously and live it truthfully in the four expressions of relationship, the precedence of the heart magnifies the fullness of our lives. We **Be** to **Do** to **Have**.

LONELY: APATHY AND LONELINESS

No matter the means we use to prevent ourselves from experiencing loss, vulnerability, wounds, rejections, and the craving for life, we are eventually led to a prison of apathy if we are unable to surrender to the voice of our hearts. Apathy means that we have found a way to be removed from the pain of life within us. The misuse of the will to dominate the heart brings us to the isolation and torpor of apathy, squashing the heart into a small space and covering it with stones. In apathy our kinship with others is denied. We are alone. Love and hate are not opposites, for each speak in their own ways of being alive, being affected by life and it mattering. Apathy and love are the true opposites, as apathy becomes our attempt not to be affected at all. It blocks the care, connection, passion, pain, and desire of love. The choice: To live, love, and lead a life with all its struggles, beauties, and drudgery, or to build an existence of distancing from everything that speaks to life, including your very being.

- SHAME -

Healthy shame, the feeling that comes with the dependency we are born into, moves us towards the relationships we were created to seek. Shame reveals how we are created as dependent, which never changes as we age. Human beings, however, are the only creatures who can attempt to deny our relational makeup. While life follows its own course, which is always larger than our own attempts to control it, we can pretend to exist in a way other than how we are made. The rejection of dependency is a declaration of insanity, denying one's selfhood, the pushing away of the very heart of who one is. We are created to live fully in relationship, knowing ourselves as human, knowing others to be like us, and knowing God as Creator with us. Healthy shame simply exposes this truth. And every child whose heart is harmed has a tendency to distance from their dependency, developing shame's impairment: toxic shame.

SHAME: SHAME AND NEEDINESS

There are essentially three ways we can find of relating to the inborn neediness that healthy shame leads us to: dependence, independence, and codependence. Healthy shame is the "neediness" feeling that leads us to a life giving and affirming dependence of others, God, and creation itself. We need the emotional and spiritual food that gratifies the relational nature of our hearts. Healthy shame allows one to express the tears and laughter of life without feeling contempt for their heart. The child, for example, whose heart is affirmed and confirmed tends to grow into a person who moves towards living fully, loving deeply, and leading well.

On the other hand, independence means having a fantasy of being without a need for relationship with others and God. In trying to remain independent, we attempt to overcome neediness itself. We are made to become independent from tyranny, but not independent from how we are made. Independence from tyranny occurs through dependence on others and God.

Finally, codependence is rooted in a belief that I must pay to be loved by performing well, which creates an anxiety-based set of actions. In codependence, we are tyrannized by the mistaken belief that my performance garners love and care. Codependence is also, somewhat ironically, an attempt at independence as it carries with it the belief that one has the power to perform well enough on one's own to be loved. It will always exhaust and create great resentment.

SHAME: SHAME AS THE GROUND FROM WHICH WE GROW

We are born assuming that how we are created is what our caregivers want us to be. It also has in it the "unthought" assumption that caregivers and others are the same as the child, that is made the same way. A child has no comparison but their own experience, and therefore, the child reaches out of neediness as natural or normal, as if to say, "Of course, you wish to meet me in every way as I am." We do not perform for love; we simply present ourselves as in need of love. We simply reach for the food. Shame accepts that we are human, so we bring to life and love the confession of our makeup—feelings, needs, desire, longings, and hope. Caregivers must have their own healthy shame awareness to accept the presentation of the child's neediness. If the caregivers and child can match, even imperfectly, shame begins the awareness that through attachment to ourselves, others and God, we grow into discovering the full expression of our generative creativity. We give ourselves to making, tending, growing, expanding, living, loving, and leading, i.e., growing into who we are created to become and doing what we are created to do.

SHAME: CORE SENTENCES OF HEALTHY SHAME

Healthy shame is the beginning of humility and risk taking. In growing our awareness of inborn neediness and how alike we all are in heart, shame awakens the following:

- *I need you and you need me.*
- *I make mistakes and you do, too.*
- *I don't have all the answers, but I have some and so do you. Let's share.*
- *I'm not God; you aren't God. We are human and in need of God.*

These four statements are general recognitions of the humility, empathy, and equality that are the basis for bringing full-hearted people together. These statements allow us to share our abilities and talents because what one person isn't skilled in, another person will be. They also allow us to accept each other as fallible and gifted. Moreover, these statements allow us to find our strength in relationship. In the neediness of healthy shame, we find we are empowered through relationship to live fully, love deeply, and lead well. In relationship with our selves, others, and God, we find the fullness of life. And we are lead to this relational way of being through the experience of healthy shame that makes us aware of how needy we are for others and God.

SHAME: THE GROWTH OF HEALTHY SHAME

Healthy shame is a remarkably generative feeling. Out of healthy shame grows some tremendously important characteristics of full-hearted people: empathy, conscience, self-awareness, and the ability to seek and extend forgiveness. The recognition of oneself as a dependent human creature grows into the ability to have empathy for others who are equally vulnerable and in need of relationship. This growth in the awareness of our shared neediness produces conscience as we grow and mature. Conscience is developed out of the recognition that if we know what hurts and harms us, we also know what can hurt and harm another. Simply, as we are conscious of our own pain and pleasure, we can identify with another's experience. If we don't know ourselves as feeling creatures, however, we will not see, accept, or care about another's pain because we deny our own. Finally, the development of conscience through empathy leads to an all-important experience called forgiveness — both giving and seeking. Forgiveness can only occur through the ability to identify with another person. We need to forgive and be forgiving because it allows us to live in relational fulfillment, allowing us to draw closer and do more together than we can apart. A hallmark of emotional and spiritual maturity is our ability to seek forgiveness and forgive.

SHAME: SHAME AND THE FELLOWSHIP OF CLUMSINESS

Life takes a lifetime to learn how to live. The best we ever become at living is like a giraffe running on ice. We are forever clumsy. Healthy shame invites us to know and admit our humanity. Shame, the neediness feeling, is a required course to receive a full education in living fully. We find our beginnings in need and our fulfillment in need — to be fully human is humbling, as we are dependent creatures. In spite of what we are often taught, self-sufficiency, independence, and power do not bring fulfillment. We need each other and God. If you are sad, for example, and I know and accept the sadness in me, I can be with you. If I am sad and you know and accept the sadness in you, you can be with me. However, if one of us hates the sadness within our selves, we will have to do something with one another's sadness: defend against it, mock it, numb it, and so on. Being with someone is extremely powerful and is impossible without the ability to humbly accept oneself as in need of others. Humility brought about by healthy shame opens the door to fulfillment and liberates us from the tyranny of refusing how we are made. Learning how to live out of one's sense of healthy shame is an educational course that requires constant refreshment, as it is remarkably hard to do. We need to begin each day with the admission of our humanity and move into the day from there.

SHAME: DISTORTION OF HEALTHY SHAME

When life's tragedy occurs, and it comes to us all, we often are told and even demanded not to need others, feel too deeply, desire too much, long for more, or hope in spite of reality. This rejection of how we are created triggers an awful condition called self-contempt or toxic shame. Toxic shame is contempt for our emotional and spiritual make up, which is the birthplace of self-care, self-acceptance, our need for others, and the expression of self-worth. If we are taught to reject our hearts by those around us when life happens, we have to develop rules and regulations that attempt to control and dominate the heart. These rules and regulations almost always, one way or another, heap contempt on the heart for continuing to feel, need, desire, long, and hope. The mission of our lives becomes following the rules that never allow us to reveal our hearts to anyone, even ourselves. Doing life "right" can quickly take the place of doing it truthfully. Rules about our God-created makeup supersede the relational expression that allows us to respond to the way life works with our hearts. Toxic shame bullies us into believing that we are defective and worthless unless we perform up to some level of perceived perfection — the perfection of invulnerability. And this, of course, we can never do. In toxic shame, clumsy becomes failure, taking a lifetime to learn how to live becomes inadequacy, and being human becomes disgusting.

SHAME: THE GREAT SADNESS REVISITED

The great sadness for us all is that in the condition called toxic shame we hide ourselves, we hide from each other, and we hide from God behind walls of performance, judgment, perfectionism, and apathy. Our demands upon our selves to have control, be invulnerable, become perfect, and to stop caring block us from the freedom of living a life of heart. In hiding, we are constrained by being forced to use most of our energy burying the heart of who we are behind a myriad of masks. Schematically, toxic shame wrecks relationship with ourselves (I secretly hate me), with others (I secretly judge you as rejecting me unless I perform for you), and with God (I believe God cannot care about me unless I perform). Toxic shame poisons the system of heart, isolating everyone from everyone.

Even in the midst of toxic shame's wreckage, we cannot stop being made for fulfillment in relationship. Only facing ourselves, feeling our feelings, telling the truth about our lives, and giving this truth to the process God made gratifies our hearts and meets our needs. Tragically, a return to healthy shame requires admitting heartache and heartbreak. Only facing ourselves, feeling our feelings, telling the truth about our lives, and giving it to the process God made, gratifies our hearts and meets our needs. In the surrender of our humanity, the very heart of us, we lose the demand of our own perfection and allow healthy shame to come home. Ironically, the solution to toxic shame is the reemergence of healthy same, which sets us free to live fully as human beings.

SHAME: JESUS AND SHAME

Jesus was vitally invested in and drawn to anyone who had the "faith of a child," or the willingness to acknowledge their neediness and the hope that someone could meet them in their neediness. Jesus starts with the hope that brings us to the vulnerable requests that children are capable of expressing. The "faith of a child" is a description of living out of healthy shame. This faith evidences an open doorway into the heart. It allows us to surrender to our need for help. Jesus knew what he was doing and how life works. We can surrender to his teaching. The choice: To surrender to how we are made and become who we are made to be, or attempt to create our selves, performing our way right to the grave, having never lived because we never would.

- GUILT -

Guilt grows out of healthy shame, and healthy shame allows me to acknowledge neediness, experience humility, identify limitations, admit mistakes, weep in sadness, wish for better, and grow in empathy and conscience as a human being. Here is how healthy shame and guilt connect. I hurt when I fall. You probably hurt when you fall. If I push you to make you fall, I have guilt because I can see what your pain would be like. You have heard the Golden Rule. We are drawn together through it. Do unto others as you would have them do unto you. It starts with the recognition that we are created alike. We are not guilty for having feelings. We have guilt when we do actions or make plans that harm who we are created to be or harm another like us.

GUILT: FALSE GUILT

We are neither guilty for having feelings, nor are we guilty when someone else has feelings. As human beings, we are unable to "fix" the feelings either we or another person have. Most of us, however, are raised to believe that we are responsible for other people's feelings, moods, thoughts, and even actions. This powerful core belief instigates a false guilt or toxic shame for not having the power to fix others. Sadly, many of us spend much of our lives attempting to be forgiven for not being able to change the feelings, moods, thoughts and actions of other people. We cannot do the impossible, for we are not God. False guilt is often a cover story for the sadness we feel in recognizing our limitations in our desire to help those that we love. This cover story tells us that one day — if we behave good enough, say the right words, do the right things — we will finally be able to fix the feelings of those we care about. We use stories about "one day" to distract us from the feelings of powerlessness we feel when confronted with the limits of our ability to help others. Beneath the veneer of false guilt are a whole host of feelings worth exploring and sharing.

GUILT: RESPONSIBILITY AND GUILT

We are response able **for** our actions, and guilt moves us to accept responsibility for our actions. To deal with guilt requires courage, the sensitivity of one's heart, and a desire of the heart to participate fully in life. When we participate in life fully, we will also be confronted with our capacity to cause harm to those we care about. Guilt, the feeling that sensitizes us to our fallibility and allows us to seek forgiveness, is part of our heart's response ability, as it allows us to acknowledge harm done. Our response ability to acknowledge harm leads us to taking responsibility for our actions and toward seeking forgiveness. No matter how sensitive to our potential for harm we become, we will always be works in progress, never arriving at any destination of completion. As works in progress, we will always be capable of great good and significant harm. There is a famous stanza of *The Serenity Prayer* by Reinhold Niebuhr that can be paraphrased to fit to our condition of remaining response able in a life of imperfection: God, grant us serenity in grieving into acceptance what we cannot change, a heart of courage to step into what we can change, and the wisdom of heart's sensitivity to discern the difference.

GUILT: THE GRANDEUR OF GOD'S FORGIVENESS

A grand hallmark of being human is the ability to seek forgiveness. We will never get beyond the "practice" of life as long as we live on the earth, so we need to become great at empathically acknowledging mistakes, harm, and sin. Remember, the best we can ever do is clumsy. We are not to use the facts of life and our imperfection to excuse our failure, however. The reality of our clumsiness is to be used to admit our failures, seek God to do what we cannot do, and to live the freedom of being fully human in relationship with the God who does for us what we can never do for ourselves. A most humbling human experience is receiving mercy and love as a clumsy, forgiven person. Clumsiness never ends, the need for amends never ends, and, thankfully, neither does God's forgiveness. In forgiveness, we who are made of dust (humus/humility), are touched by God who created us and loves us.

GUILT: THE BLESSING OF HEALTHY SHAME AND GUILT

Healthy shame allows us to discover guilt. Out of our confession and acceptance of our selves as in need of our hearts, others, and God, we can become aware of our selves as clumsy, have empathy with others, and experience conscience before others and God. Toxic shame, contempt for being human, blocks the relational repair that guilt can offer. Guilt says, "I'm sorry I did _____. I have sorrow. Please forgive me" Toxic shame, on the other hand, says, "I'm sorry I did _____. I do not believe you can forgive me, but I will do everything to make it up to you, if you will not reject me." Guilt is moved by a desire to love and is the pain and regret of not doing so. Toxic shame is moved by the desire to take action so that we will not receive what we think we deserve. Guilt is moved by the desire for mercy, the admission that we cannot deserve what we wish to receive — freedom of knowing we are forgiven and loved.

GUILT: CYCLE OF TOXIC SHAME VS. PATHWAY OF GUILT

The difference between toxic shame and guilt is that one is a cycle and the other a path; one takes us somewhere, while the other returns us to where we started ad nauseam. In toxic shame, we just start the cycle of trying harder to be worthy of love again and again, as we are compelled by a fear of rejection. This cycle of attempting to be more than human will always bring us back to judging our selves and others, preventing us from experiencing the mercy and grace brought about by guilt and forgiveness. Toxic shame traps us in a cycle of taking action to make us not feel bad about our selves. While this cycle works for a time, i.e., offers temporary relief, it always demands that we do the next thing, because we will start to doubt the status our actions brought us soon enough. In toxic shame, we are stuck in always not finding acceptance, as our lives are based on having to perform to get love; hence, to stop performing would be to give up on love.

On the other hand, the pathway of guilt sets us free to remain fully human in all of our imperfections. If we have empathy, we will take actions based on our experience of guilt. The path way of guilt puts one in route to seeking reconciliation and life in a community. In this world, unfortunately, we see much more acting in toxic shame than we see taking action based in the response ability of guilt. We see more pride than sorrow, more grandiosity than humility, more pretending than presence, and more relief seeking than living again. The choice: To become human, become our selves, receive the mercy of love in the midst of all of our foibles and failures, and give the same of love to others. Or, we can regret being human, run away from our imperfections, and miss our lives fluctuating between apologizing for not being perfect and priding our selves on trying to be good.

- GLAD -

Gladness comes to us as an outcome of being adept at the other seven feelings. If we become adept at allowing and using the other seven feelings, we become glad and experience a general sense of well-being. When we face and feel life with hope, longings, desire, and needs, we will have a multitude of celebrations, minute and large, and a multitude of losses, large and minute. Even so, we will have participated in the experience of creation, we will have been fully alive to all that life had to offer. Everything that has life in it seeks its fulfillment and completion. It seeks its gladness, so to speak. We are created to have an expression of gladness as we move on the path of fulfillment to live fully, love deeply, and lead well in a way that leaves something behind.

GLAD: PART OF GLADNESS IS PAIN

Again, gladness is a result of being adept at feeling the other seven feelings: guilt, hurt, shame, anger, sad, fear, and lonely. We live towards fulfillment by taking emotional and spiritual risks with our heart's desire, longings, and hope. With reaching, risking, caring, and growing comes inevitable struggle. Remember, we live in a broken place with heavenly imaginations. This place is one of tragedy in which we struggle to connect our experience to the hope, faith and love of God's faithfulness. Humans cannot have fulfillment without pain, and no celebration exists without it either, for even celebrations have ends. Life to the full is actually lived between how well we celebrate and grieve. Willingness to connect and grieve the inevitable losses brought on by attachment make up the fulfilled life on this earth. By admitting our condition of powerlessness over how we are created as emotional and spiritual creatures, surrendering our heart's makeup to God's process, and struggling daily with acceptance, we can live fully and well. Through living this process over and over again, we are able to derive an experience of gladness from our lives.

GLAD: REVISITING THE RISK OF LOVE

If we love well, allowing ourselves to be "all in," we will undoubtedly have experiences that bring pain to our lives. Our perseverance in life is built upon our capacity to continue to love even in the midst of the pain that love inevitably leads to. Relationships require and bring pain as a part of life and as a result of love. For example, the moment we begin to attach to, care about, and invest in our children, fear, worry, heartache, hurt and powerlessness come into our lives. Along with, of course, joy, warmth, care, and celebration. There is such gladness and such pain with love. Learning to hold this tension well is a hallmark of living well and growth in being a full-hearted person. Being willing and able to cry or laugh at any moment takes a lifetime to learn. Taking the risk of connecting to people and places with our hearts brings us to our most vulnerable places. Without the ability to expose our most vulnerable places to the process of life on life's terms, however, we will miss our lives. Love is a risk precisely because we can live without loving, and living a life of love is an all or nothing venture.

GLAD: THE COST OF GLADNESS

When a child grows up and departs home, if there is relational connection between the child and the caretakers, there will be sadness, loneliness, fear, and a host of other feelings. And this happens when the separation with a child is proper and good and healthy. With intimate connection, the pain of proper separation is full of pain, because it is admitted, surrendered to, and accepted. We will miss our children, while we also have gratitude that this growing person can leave us and venture into their own lives — joy with sadness. We will miss our children and be grateful to be able to miss our children, if we surrender to an emotional and spiritual life. We will experience the gratitude or grace of being fully alive. We find the gratitude of life in the experience of risking to love in this life. Life is painful no matter how we relate to it. Connection to life emotionally and spiritually is painful, as well. And love is the paramount expression of a heart fully participating in life. The greater the love, the greater the care, the greater the risk of pain and loss.

GLAD: ALLOWING GLADNESS

Gladness occurs as an outcome of the courage to feel, which is the beginning of what is required to "keep heart." It is birthed and grown over and over again out of one's willingness to fully participate in life. And fully participating in life begins by admitting and surrendering to how we are made as emotional and spiritual creatures. Courage has its genesis in birth and its solidification in relationship with trusted others. Children are born with the desperation of desire and the courage to express it, and we are made to mature and keep this same desire and courage. This desire and inborn capacity to reach towards living fully moves a person towards gladness. We grow into using pain to express our desire for life and love. We use pain to seek resolution in disconnection, disorder, and discomfort. We develop high tolerance for pain and yet have the sensitivity to pain to reach for its resolution. We become resolved to live fully in a world over which we are powerless, because powerlessness does not remove us from choice or potency to respond to our hearts and life. We have found that all feelings can bring us the gifts that allow us to remain vitally connected to life and love. This surrender to how we are created and living out of how we are created leads us to gladness, a form of having competence and confidence in a world over which we do not have control.

GLAD: ADMISSION OF OUR CONDITION TO HAVE GLADNESS

Jesus spoke so beautifully and frighteningly when he said that we must change and become as a child to enter the kingdom of heaven. Instead of using will power to stifle our heart's desire so that we won't have pain, we are to give back over to the heart of desire. We are to return our will back over to the One who created us to desire, and to do so passionately and imaginatively. We are to use will to live a life of desire, not block it. Life is often tragic, and God is faithful in the midst of hardship. The passion of our hearts, the struggle for life, the capacity to hope, and the unavoidable expense of its vulnerabilities brings us to gladness. The almost unutterable experience of love is the ultimate gladness.

GLAD: IMPAIRED GLADNESS

Impaired gladness is an attempt to experience fulfillment without having to feel fully. Eating a bunch of donuts will absolutely comfort us for a time, but they do not gratify the heart. An affair of any kind is an illegitimate form of getting legitimate needs met. While an affair temporarily stops the need to deal with heartache, it doesn't gratify the heart's desire to live in genuine passion, intimacy, and integrity. In short, impaired gladness is the sensuous and sensual attempt to have fulfillment without the heart being fully present or involved. The tragedy of this impairment is that we become controlled by happenstance, or happenings, continuing to focus on that thing that will make us happy, which, ironically, is the escape from the fulfillment of gladness. Gladness has room in it for other feelings. It is so ironic that happiness can become the enemy of gladness and its resultant joy. If our hearts are not present to allow us to be receptive and truthful, anything we bring into ourselves—food, religion, sex, exciting experiences, plans for the future, even—will leave us temporarily satisfied but not fulfilled.

A RETURN TO THE BEGINNING OF THESE PARAGRAPHS

To return to the essential beginnings of ourselves and keeping heart, we are created as emotional and spiritual creatures, created to do one thing in life: live fully. We can only live fully by being in relationship with our true selves, others, and God. A human being's full presence and joy comes from returning to the truth of how we are made and surrendering to the process of how life works. A human being's greatest power is the capacity to refuse how we are created. We can destroy ourselves through a refusal of our hearts. Our greatest fulfillment comes from being in relationship with the One who made us, and then living this relational capacity in our daily lives with ourselves and others. The choice: To surrender to our pre-design as relational creatures, or to refuse to surrender and survive as a prisoner of self-will and denial.

SUMMARY

Feelings are the living, dynamic truth about being human, and are made to be what we use our thoughts to think about. We are able to locate ourselves in space and time truthfully by using our heads to express our hearts, unless we are in refusal about what it's like to be human. If we are in denial or in revolt against the healthy shame of being a person, we have to suppress our hearts through the use of our wills or our heads. This act of suppression keeps us running from the emotional and spiritual experiences of our hearts. A person who hates their humanity answers God's question to Adam in Genesis, "Where are you?" by saying, "Standing behind the tree," or "Hiding in the dark," or "I hate you for asking." We can only be met in the truth, the nakedness of our emotional and spiritual cores, by reaching into our hearts and handing the truth over to God and others. Through willingness, patience, work, and time, we receive the gifts that the tools of feelings, needs, desire, longings and hope bring.

CHAPTER EIGHT

THE EQUATION FOR THE GIFTS OF FEELINGS

ooooo

WILLINGNESS + PATIENCE + WORK + TIME= GIFTS OF FEELINGS

WILLINGNESS

Willingness is the energy of allowing our hearts to be given over to hoping again, even though past experiences have taught us to think of hope as foolish.

PATIENCE

Patience is the ability to persevere amidst the struggle of living fully, a capacity to keep caring and believing in the truth of God's faithfulness in spite of heartache. Patience bears the burden of hope—the weight of wishing and believing. In the capacity to wait well while continuing to move with desire, we continue to express hope with the daily surrender of our lives. Sometimes patience is like a woman in childbirth, writhing in pain and anticipation, while other times patience is the waiting when nothing seems to occur at all.

WORK

Work is the surrender of our whole selves to the experience of what matters to us. We bring our hands, head, and heart to our lives. Work will be done most completely when we are where and with whom we hunger to be with. While most people believe that work goes on outside the house, the greatest beauty of work is to be done inside the home.

TIME

Time is what moves whether we participate in our lives or not. Whether we live or not, time goes on. To participate in our lives, we must use time by taking up space emotionally and spiritually in the present. It means to live from the inside-out, to be known, and to connect with heart. Willingness, patience, and work combine to allow us to be present within each moment.

THE EQUATION AND ITS OUTCOME

The outcome of the equation — willingness + patience + work + time = gifts of the feelings — opens the door for us to experience life fully. The gifts that come through daily surrender to being an emotional and spiritual creature will deliver us gifts that foster living fully, loving deeply, and leading well.

Sad brings us to acceptance

Anger brings us to passion

Hurt brings us to healing and courage

Lonely brings us to intimacy

Fear brings us to faith and wisdom

Shame brings us to humility

Guilt brings us to forgiveness and freedom

Glad brings us to joy combined with sadness

An

INVITATION TO DREAM

ooooo

The door of the heart shuts where the pearls have small sweet flames coming from their tops, cushioned in sparrows' down and butterfly dust, where pumpkin seeds and trumpet vine blooms circle the feast of light; June bugs wings still glisten green there and a white clover chain makes scent; I can smell the hope smoke puff up because the ones in the room, one or a multitude, just simply blew out the sacrifice of life and still the firefly flickered one more time before smeared across the table top in the dark, leaving a trail like a comet in a tiny universe that crosses the darkness and is gone. Love is such a freak, wrested by the descent into the decent and stomped into pissed-oil by the apes of blood lust. And still we, you and I, if you have the slightest memory—and if you have come this far, you do—we go with the rains washed into the culverts without a fight because courage has tears of pursuit wrapped around our hope buried in the memory place that we could not exile even when we knew self-hatred would be the reward of revolution until the grief that came with the valor's limp let us walk the long walk home to the war in which not one of us gives up.

SALUTATION

ooooo

ONE LAST RECOGNITION

These statements are somewhat cursory about feelings, needs, desire, longings, and hope. They speak of our pre-design. They speak to us as created beings. They allow us to struggle with the surrender of our hearts to how we are made and how life is. They allow us to give our selves to a God who is present, and they allow us to struggle with creation and our dreams of living. If we are raised to keep heart, our thoughts can be used to express our hearts. Our thoughts are responsive rather than reactive, and our behavior will express the truth about our selves congruently. Our spirituality in life can be explored and struggled with openly to know the Presence of God and recognize life as more than survival; our responses to our environments will be with boundaries more than defensiveness because we are able to live in response ability; and our physiology will not be dictated by anxiety as the controlling force of our lives, and the suffering that it dictates in all our decisions. It really is a small world "full of laughter and full of tears, full of hopes and full of fears," ("It's a Small World"). We will never have complete peace, home, safety, and justice this side of the heaven, but we were created for it. Life is tragic and God is faithful. We are born desperate with desire and with the courage to express it, which allows us to be able to live fully in a tragic place if we keep heart. We are created for relationship, and have full life in relationships. We are made to love and have to fight to keep it. We are made to lead, and ultimately only people of heart are true leaders—because they have the character to desire truly what can be for others' good.

Blessings,

Live fully, love deeply, lead well.

Sentio ergo sum.

Keep Heart.

About the Author

CHIP DODD

ooooo

Chip Dodd, PhD, is a teacher, trainer, author, and counselor, who has been working in the field of recovery and redemption for over 30 years. It is the territory in which people can return to living the way we are created to live— where we can move from mere survival to living fully, from isolation to loving deeply, and from controlling to leading others well.

In 1996 Chip founded the Center for Professional Excellence in Nashville, where he continues the work of helping people recover their lives.

With his clinical experience, love of storytelling, and passion for living fully, Chip developed a way of seeing and expressing one's internal experience called the Spiritual Root System™. It expresses the essential heart of human beings and gives practical tools to live fully, love deeply, and lead well.

About

SAGE HILL

ooooo

Sage Hill is a social impact organization founded by Chip Dodd, committed to helping others see who they are made to be so they can do what they are made to do.

Wherever life has you, we're here to help you keep heart. We offer recovery and addiction treatment programs, therapeutic counseling, leadership development intensives, corporate consulting, staff retreats, teaching resources, and more. Visit us online for more information.

CPENASHVILLE.COM

The JourneyPure Center for Professional Excellence is a multidisciplinary treatment center for professional men who want to recover their lives, their passions, and their integrity from the effects of addiction, depression, anxiety, and other behavioral problems.

SAGE HILL COUNSELING.COM

When life doesn't work, Sage Hill Counseling is here to help. We offer counseling for individuals, couples, families, children/adolescents, and group therapies to help you heal, grow, and mature. Sage Hill Counseling centers are currently located in Nashville, TN, and Memphis, TN.

SAGE HILL RESOURCES.COM

Sage Hill Resources is dedicated to producing materials that help you keep heart. All of our resources use the wisdom of the Spiritual Root System™ to help you gain a deeper understanding of your heart, which can lead to more authentic relationship with yourself, others, and God.

SAGE HILL TRAINING.COM

Sage Hill Training is a transformational learning experience created to benefit people-helpers from all walks of life to live fully, love deeply and lead well. Specifically designed to profoundly benefit you on both a professional and personal level, this relationship-centered training will help you better serve others with passion, wisdom, and integrity.

WAKE UP AND GO HOME TO WHO YOU ARE MADE TO BE.

SAGE HILL
A SOCIAL IMPACT ORGANIZATION

The Voice of the Heart

COMPANION BIBLE STUDY

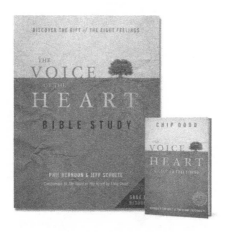

SECOND EDITION

with Companion Bible Study

In 2001, *The Voice of the Heart* began a steady journey into the lives of those looking for more. Since its initial release, *The Voice of the Heart* has been handed one friend to another and has helped thousands of people begin to speak the truth of their story and to live more fully from the heart.

AVAILABLE ONLINE AT WWW.SAGEHILLRESOURCES.COM

The
NEEDS OF THE HEART

The Second Root of the Spiritual Root System™

Without knowing and expressing our needs, relationship with God and others suffers. As a complement to *The Voice of the Heart*, Chip Dodd invites readers to explore the needs we are created to have so that we can live fully.

The
PERFECT LOSS

A Different Kind of Happiness

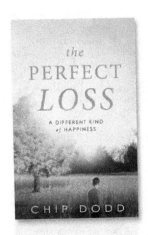

Through the use of story, experience, knowledge, and Scripture, we follow Chip Dodd as he shows us how to walk the path toward a life of passion, intimacy and integrity—leaving a legacy that passes life forward to those we love and beyond.

Though the fig tree does not bud and there are no grapes on the vines, though the olive crop fails and the fields produce no food, though there are no sheep in the pen and no cattle in the stalls, yet I will rejoice in the LORD.

—Habakkuk 3:17-18

USING THE BEATITUDES, THE AUTHOR SHOWS US THE EIGHT MOVEMENTS WE ALL MUST MAKE IF WE ARE TO LIVE FULLY.

AVAILABLE ONLINE AT WWW.SAGEHILLRESOURCES.COM

LIVE FULLY, LOVE DEEPLY, LEAD WELL

Meditations on Passion, Intimacy, & Integrity

We are created as emotional and spiritual creatures designed to live fully, love deeply, and lead well.

These small books will help you think a little, wonder some, and ponder more. The words can settle into your heart in such a way that you can be reminded of who you are made to be and have more recovery of your life.

Be replenished to live fully each day.

ANTHEM TO THE INVISIBLE

"A book ahead of its time."

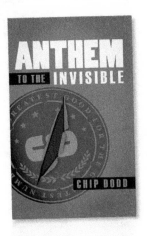

An allegory that speaks truths we are trained not to see, and we wish we could hide from. It sends us into the future in which metaphor and science have collided into a new materialism. We have gotten everything we ever wanted and yet the cost to the heart of who we are is its price. The unique story takes us into the mystery of our own hearts and beckons us to listen to our own cry for liberty.

AVAILABLE ONLINE AT WWW.SAGEHILLRESOURCES.COM

STAY INSPIRED, KEEP HEART

Connect with Sage Hill

Find daily inspiration, stay current on Sage Hill events, gain access to free videos, and more.

SUBSCRIBE ONLINE AT WWW.SAGEHILLRESOURCES.COM